The Chef from Rector's

The Chef from Rector's

A Selection of Culinary Columns

George Rector

COACHWHIP PUBLICATIONS
GREENVILLE, OHIO

The Chef from Rector's, by George Rector
© 2024 Coachwhip Publications

First published 1938-1939
George Rector, 1878-1947
CoachwhipBooks.com

ISBN 1-61646-595-6
ISBN-13 978-1-61646-595-7

Introduction

It would not be out of line to refer to George Rector (1878-1947) as one of America's first celebrity chefs. He came from a family of restauranteurs, with his grandfather operating hotels with restaurants in New York State. Rector's father, Charles, opened a dining room in Chicago, which became the popular Rector's Oyster House. In 1899, Charles and George opened Rector's in New York on Broadway. Though working in the restaurant, George was also studying law, but his father sent him to France for training in the Café de Paris. During the early 1900s, iterations of Rector's continued to be among the most popular restaurants in New York City, only ending upon the coming of Prohibition. George Rector wrote several cookbooks and a popular cooking column for the newspapers, had a weekly radio program (*Dining with George Rector*), and appeared on television and in at least one movie (*Every Day's a Holiday*, 1937).

See also:
ANATOMY OF A RESTAURATEUR: GEORGE RECTOR
    https://restaurant-ingthroughhistory.com/2018/07/11/anatomy-of-a-restaurateur-george-rector/

Rector's, New York City, 1899-1919
   https://www.theamericanmenu.com/2015/08/rectors.html

Rector's: The Elaine's of 1899
   https://www.toquemag.com/uncategorized/rectors-the-elaines-of-1899

Columns

January 7, 1938: Poached Eggs in Olive Oil—Eggs Bercy—Eggs and Shrimp
January 14, 1938: Chicken Marengo—Duck with Danish Stuffing—Paprika Chicken
January 21, 1938: Chicken Spanish Stew—Zabaione
January 28, 1938: Oysters—Philadelphia Pan Fried Oysters—Creamed Oysters—Crabmeat
February 4, 1938: Shredded Cabbage—Hot Slaw—Potato Salad—Meat Salad
February 11, 1938: Steak and Kidney Pie—Hungarian Goulash—Meat Loaf
February 18, 1938: Pig's Feet with Sauce Diablé—Honeycomb Tripe
February 25, 1938: Chicken Hash—Lamb Hash—Corned Beef Hash
March 11, 1938: Hollandaise Sauce—Crabmeat Newburg
March 18, 1938: Onion Soup—Vichyssoise—Mulligatawny—Corn Chowder
March 25, 1938: Corn Mexicaine—Fried Onion Rings—Carrots a la Vichy—Peas
April 1, 1938: Poulet Maison—Lobster a l'Americanne
April 8, 1938: Ragout of Beef a la Deutsch—New England Baked Beans

April 15, 1938: Hors d'Oeuvres—Deviled Eggs—Cheese Puffs—Shrimp in Sauce—Roquefort Cheese Mix

April 22, 1938: Minced Clams on Toast—Cumberland Sauce—Mayonnaise

April 29, 1938: Bouillabaisse Marseillaise—Salad Dressing

May 6, 1938: Martini Cocktail—Café Diablé—Maple Parfait

May 13, 1938: Lamb Kidney Stew—Spoon Bread—Yorkshire Pudding—Gingersnap Gravy

May 20, 1938: Braised Duckling with Fruit Sauce—Stuffed Lamb

May 27, 1938: Chicken Curry—Chutney—Asparagus a la Polonaise

June 3, 1938: Noodles and Ham—Veal Loaf—Lemon Mousse—Potatoes Anna

June 10, 1938: Sweetbread, Braised or Broiled—Virginia Ham

June 17, 1938: Cooking Fish in Paper—Calf's Head—Calf's Brain

June 24, 1938: Bran Bread—Shortcake—Strawberry Meringue

July 1, 1938: Aspic—Jellied Chicken Salad—Molded Salmon Salad—Fruit Salad Part Frozen—Tomato Aspic Salad

July 8, 1938: Crepes Suzette—Baked Rice and Pineapple Pudding

July 15, 1938: Stilton Cheese—Welsh Rabbit—Golden Buck—Cheese Souffle

July 22, 1938: Smoked Beef Tongue with Sauce Piquante—White Bean Puree

July 29, 1938: Chinese Omelette—Chop Suey

August 5, 1938: Peach Conde—Peach Melba—Canning Peaches

August 12, 1938: Chicken Fricassee—Southern Cornbread—Popovers—Spoon Bread—Sauce with Hard Cooked Eggs—Robert Sauce

August 19, 1938: Refrigerator Ice Cream—Frozen Eggnog—Frozen Bread Pudding

August 26, 1938: Corn Relish—Tomato Relish—Green Tomato Pickle—Pickled Crab Apples—Sweet Pickled Pears

September 2, 1938: Marinated Beef—Potato Pancakes—Potato Croquettes—New England Boiled Dinner (Corned Beef)—Corned Beef Sauce

September 9, 1938: Oysters Poulette—Oysters Au Gratin—Double-Decker Oyster Pie—Pigs in Blankets—Broiled Oysters, Cabbage Relish—Oyster and Scallop Fricassee—Cocktail Sauce

September 16, 1938: Boiled Mutton, Caper Sauce—Onion Sauce—Scotch Broth—South Down Shortcake—German Pancakes

September 23, 1938: Onion Soup Au Gratin—Broiled Halibut—Fillet of Sole, Doree—Vegetable Panache

September 30, 1938: Chicken Curry—Carrot Mold—Bien Me Sabe—Jelly Roll—Sugar Cookie

October 7, 1938: Ox Tail En Casserole—Roast Ham, Cider Sauce—Veal Cutlet Marengo—Veal Birds—Veal Chops à la Zingara

October 14, 1938: Seafood Newburg—Oyster Omelet—Codfish Puffs with Tomato Sauce

October 21, 1938: Eggs Au Beurre Noir—Egg Timbale—Eggs Florentine—Brown Betty—Hard Sauce

October 28, 1938: Consommé—Consommé Alfredo—Consommé Royal—Chicken Gumbo—Consommé Alexandria

November 4, 1938: Spaghetti Milanaise—Spaghetti Alfredo with Meat Sauce

November 11, 1938: Fillet Mignon—Horseradish Sauce—Fried Bananas—Cinnamon Layer Cake, Butter Cream Icing

November 18, 1938: Meat Balls, Creole Sauce—Baked Corned Beef Hash—Mushroom Bouchees—Canned Corn Souffle

November 25, 1938: Fillet of Sole, Marguery—Potatoes Gaufrette—Cucumber Salad with Sour Cream Dressing—Baked Prune Whip

December 2, 1938: Roast Turkey—Giblet Gravy—Savory Bread Stuffing—Sausage Stuffing—Chestnut and Raisin Stuffing—Thousand Island Dressing

December 9, 1938: Crabmeat Ravigote—Cream of Mushroom Soup—Chestnut Puree—Candied Sweet Potatoes—Marshmallow Sweet Potatoes—Spiced Cranberries—Cranberry Jelly

December 16, 1938: Escallopine of Veal Au Marsala—Clarified Butter—Blanquette of Veal—Apple Snow—Boiled Custard Sauce

December 22, 1938: Wild Duck, Roasted—Fried Hominy—Cumberland Sauce

December 30, 1938: Broiled Venison Steak—Ragout of Venison—Honey Chocolate Cake—Chocolate Icing—Sponge Baskets

January 6, 1939: Oyster Sauté—Oysters Casino—Bass Portugaise—Cheese Cake

January 13, 1939: Eggs de la Maison—Chicken Tettrazini—Shrimps à la Creole—Minced Shrimps Louisianne—Fried Shrimps, Mar Dong

January 20, 1939: Ragout of Beef, Bourgeoise—Rolled Roast, Provencal—Beef Liver, Creole—Honeycomb Tripe and Onions—Roast Forequarter of Lamb

January 27, 1939: Lamb Hash, Café de Paris—Roast Duck, Armenonville—Baked Skewered Fruit—Broiled Ducklings—Rhubarb Meringue Pie

February 3, 1939: Baked Tender Ham—Creamed Ham, Rice Border—Ham Risotto—Ham Mousse, Epicurean Sauce—Welsh Rabbit—Salmagundi Salad

February 10, 1939: Puff Paste—Napoleons—Rissoles—Compote of Fresh Fruit

February 17, 1939: Mayonnaise—Curry Mayonnaise—Russian Dressing—Thousand Island Dressing—French Dressing—Lorenzo Dressing—Vinaigrette—Roquefort Cheese Dressing—Salad Dressing

February 24, 1939: French Griddle Toast—French Toast Savory Sandwich—Omelet à la Poulard

March 3, 1939: Deviled Stuffed Crab—Roasted Guinea Hen—Roasted Guinea Hen En Casserole—Baked Alaska—Strawberry Ice Box Mousse

March 10, 1939: Sweetbreads Newburg—Wiener Schnitzel—Soft-shell Clams, Mexicano—Broiled Salmon Steak—Cheesewich—Orange Custard

March 17, 1939: Hollandaise Sauce—Grilled Sardines à la Seville—Fruit Upside Down Cake—Maple Sugar Toast

March 24, 1939: Cabbage Soup—Scrambled Codfish—Swiss Steak—Broiled Lamb Chops, Currant Sauce—Currant Mint Sauce—Baked Eggs Au Gratin—Zabaione

March 31, 1939: Broiled Lobster—Lobster Thermidor—Chicken Cacciotora—Potatoes Au Gratin—Glaze Apples

January 7, 1938

All my life, and that means a good many years, I have been interested in what is going on in the kitchen. I just can't resist poking my nose into the culinary department, no matter whether I am in a home or a restaurant.

It was only a short time ago while on a motor trip that we came to a filling station and adjoining the station was a restaurant. As I entered I was attracted by the extreme neatness of the place. No cookery odors, spotless linen on all tables, polished floors well, it was about the most inviting place of its kind I had ever seen. It was not long before I was in the kitchen. The lady cook-proprietor was then active in the preparation of the "soup du jour."

The first thing that caught my eye was a large bowl of eggs. That alone was a particular treat because I am very fond of eggs. But that wasn't all I saw. Alongside of the eggs was a stack of middle cooked ham—you know, the middle cut—and there you have that great American dish of ham and eggs.

That was my order. Now came the preparation, which almost broke my heart. The cook reached for the skillet and placed it on the hot stove. Then from a crock under a table she scooped out a large spoonful of vicious-looking drippings and the moment it went into the skillet I said, under my breath. "Ouch! There go my ham and eggs." The point is, why spoil a perfectly good dish?

POACHED EGGS IN OLIVE OIL.

The last time I was in Italy I saw prepared in the famous Alfredo's restaurant in Rome poached eggs cooked in olive oil. They were delicious. It's so easy to do. Heat the olive oil, not too hot, in a medium depth saucepan. Give the oil a whirl with a spoon just before you drop in the eggs, one at a time. When they are cooked you will see they have taken on a brownish color instead of the usual white, as when done in water. Well! I certainly enjoyed them. Try it sometime.

Last week I gave you that standard recipe for French dressing. If you want to enrich the flavor of the dressing stir thoroughly two egg yolks into a half cup of the dressing. In French dressing I have also used hard-cooked yolks which have been put through a fine sieve.

If you do not know what Eggs Bercy are, I'll tell you. They are glorified shirred eggs. Here's the way we do it:

HERE'S THE PART WHERE BERCY COMES IN.

Butter small shirred egg dishes. Break two eggs into each dish and place in a moderate oven for about 20 minutes or until they become set. Now comes the Bercy part. When the eggs are cooked (and don't forget to season them while they are cooking) place beside each two small cooked sausages and also a chicken liver which has been cooked along with the sausages.

Now for the Sauce Bercy. Extract of beef is the secret and the base of this sauce. Begin:

Heat a small can of tomato sauce. Dissolve a tablespoon of extract of beef in four tablespoons of boiling water. Add this to the tomato sauce and mix well. Season with a few grains of cayenne pepper and a pinch of salt.

Just before removing from the stove add one tablespoon of butter. Pour this sauce over the eggs, and then you have eggs a la Bercy without paying anything extra for the a la.

RECIPE FROM BELGIUM USES EGGS AND SHRIMP. Over in Belgium I came across a splendid egg dish. It contains shrimp and I found it very tasty, so I am passing it on to you. It calls for six hard cooked eggs chopped but not too fine, about it in this way:

Melt two tablespoons of butter in a saucepan, add the chopped eggs, one tablespoon of finely chopped parsley, one-half teaspoon of dry mustard, one-half cup of cooked shrimp, one-half pint of cream, two tablespoons of dry sherry, a very light pinch of cayenne pepper, and one half teaspoon of salt.

The above ingredients must be thoroughly heated and gently stirred. I would suggest serving the combination on triangles of toast.

January 14, 1938

You know what I would like to see? A contest! To determine the most popular food in America. From what I have gathered at my cooking schools throughout the country, I think I've got it! Anyhow, I'll put the question up to you. What is the food that you will find on the highways, byways, at county fairs, ball games, and race tracks? What's the answer? HOT DOGS, of course.

At a football game last fall I saw a terrific consumption of them all around me, including one for myself. I don't think I would be very far off if I made a statement that, from a poundage standpoint, the hot dog is the best seller.

Every one knows how to serve them. The simplest and best way is to heat them thoroughly in very hot water. You can't glorify the hot dog, but the other day I saw in a magazine a recipe that was most unusual. They were called frankfurts—without any a la tacked on. Here's how it read: "Split them, fill with a strip of Swiss cheese and sweet relish. Fasten with toothpicks. bake in hot oven until brown. Serve on toast atop sautéed pineapple slices."

How would you like that? Beer is the natural beverage for frankfurts, but I think a chocolate soda would go better with the above concoction.

No one enjoys good food more than I do, but there is such a thing as dressing it up too much. Simple dishes with the proper seasonings cannot be improved upon.

SALTING STEAK BEFORE COOKING MAKES IT TOUGH.

A fine sirloin or porterhouse steak can be ruined by putting salt on it before broiling. Salt will toughen it every time. Rub a little oil over the steak just before you place it under the broiler flame to brown lightly on both sides, and then season with salt and pepper. It's the same principle when, roasting a turkey, chicken, or leg of lamb. Sear it first to seal in the juices.

I like the way a French chef does a certain chicken dish. In fact, I am very fond of a great many French dishes. Perhaps it is because I was brought up in the French cuisine where I served my apprenticeship in the famous Cafe de Paris and Marquery's, in Paris, France. I want you to know about this chicken dish I have in mind. It is called chicken Marengo.

You will want a fairly good-sized frying chicken. After it is cleaned, disjoint it to make about eight pieces. Pour in the frying pan four or five tablespoons of oil or the same quantity of butter. Brown the pieces of chicken, season with salt and pepper.

Now add one dozen small white onions, one dozen medium-sized mushrooms, and a button of garlic. Add to the chicken the pulp of one small can of tomatoes or four fresh tomatoes peeled and quartered. Cover the frying pan and cook in a moderate oven for about one and one-half hours, or until chicken is tender. While cooking add a cupful of good stock and baste occasionally.

THAT GARLIC! DON'T FORGET TO TOSS IT AWAY.

When the chicken is done remove to a hot platter. To the sauce remaining in the pan add one-half cup white wine, Sauterne type. Let this sauce reduce a little bit and then pour in over the chicken, but don't forget to remove the button of garlic. Too much sauce will give the appearance of a stew, which it is not. You will enjoy the flavor of the vegetables cooked with the chicken.

A roast domestic duck is mighty good eating, especially when you use a Danish stuffing which I have had in my files for a long time. The butcher will clean and dress the duck, and while he's about it tell him to chop off the neck. When you get the bird in the kitchen sprinkle the inside with salt and pepper and then make way for this savory Danish stuffing; it's good, believe me:

Chop finely one small onion and brown it lightly in butter. Season with one-half teaspoon of salt and a light pinch of cayenne pepper, also add one cup finely chopped celery, one and one-half cups of dry bread crumbs, one cup of prune pulp, and one cup of tart apples finely chopped. Mix thoroughly the above ingredients and moisten with one-half cup of melted butter.

Now fill the bird with the stuffing, sew up opening, and truss. Rub the duck with a little oil, and place on its back in an open roasting pan, preferably on a rack. Roast in moderate oven (350°), allowing 25 minutes to the pound. During the cooking baste it every now and then. Ducks contain considerable fat, so it is not necessary to pour water in the pan.

MME. SCHOENER IS FREE-HANDED WITH PAPRIKA.

I think you will agree with me that extensive traveling in this country as well as abroad on a mission to find out how a certain dish is prepared is more important than reading about it in a cookbook. Well, when I saw that very famous woman proprietor of the justly famous Schoener's restaurant in Vienna prepare paprika chicken it seemed to taste better than any I ever had. You ought to see her souse it with paprika and that is what makes this very delectable dish. Madame Schooner is a cook, and make no mistake about it.

Here's how she goes about it:

Cut a frying chicken in six or eight pieces. Dredge these with flour and season with salt and pepper. Brown the pieces on both sides in a sauté pan, using butter or the cooking fat you prefer. A cup of good stock is added, also a button of garlic, and now here is where the paprika makes its appearance. I saw Mme. Schoener put in two tablespoons of paprika. Don't let that shock you. It makes the dish.

Let the chicken go on cooking for about an hour. Remove to a hot platter and to the remaining sauce in the pan add one cup of cream. Heat, stir, and then pour over the chicken. If the sauce is not thick enough, make a paste of a little flour and cold water to thicken it.

January 21, 1938

I am very fond of some Spanish dishes, especially the way they cook chicken. San Sebastian was the summer resort for royalty and the place of business for bull fighters. I do not offhand remember the name of that fashionable hotel overlooking the Bay of Biscay, but, more important, I met the Spanish chef, who spoke French, so we got along all right. The chef told me about his chicken specialty. He described it to me "blow by blow," and then we sat down and ate it.

CHICKEN SPANISH STEW.

The name of the dish is just plain chicken Spanish stew and it contains a great many ingredients, so follow the recipe closely:

- 4 tablespoons olive oil
- 2 onions (sliced)
- 1 cup canned tomatoes (pulp)
- ⅓ cup finely chopped pimientos
- 1 button garlic (finely chopped)
- ½ cup of peas
- 1 frying chicken (disjointed)
- ½ lb rice (uncooked)
- 1 cup canned corn (dry pack)

1 teaspoon saffron
1 teaspoon salt
2 cups good stock
⅓ teaspoon cayenne pepper
1 tablespoon finely chopped parsley

Now there you have the ingredients. I hope you have a large earthen casserole, the kind with a handle on it. That's the proper cooking utensil to use. Heat the oil in this casserole and add the garlic, onions, and tomatoes, and cook for about five minutes. Now come the peas, the corn, the rice, and pepper, all to be added to the tomatoes and onions and stirred gently.

Season the chicken with a little salt and pepper and add to the cooking vegetables along with the saffron (you get your saffron in a drug store). Have you ever noticed how often the word "add" is used in recipes? Well, now, go ahead and add a cup of good stock, cover the casserole, and cook slowly for one hour and a half or until the chicken is tender. About every 20 minutes take a look at the chicken and give it a gentle stir. If it has the appearance of being not moist enough add a little more stock. It's a stew, all right, but you don't want it too soupy. Just before serving sprinkle over the top the chopped parsley and the pimientos.

Now there is a meal in itself. You have meat, vegetables, and a delicious sauce all in one. This Spanish chef was certainly a grand cook and knew good food.

So it is with a restaurateur and I have said it a hundred times: Show me a restaurant man who enjoys and knows good food and I'll come back and say he can't help but run a good restaurant. That also applies to the housewife. If she is indifferent about her cooking it's bound to show up in the food. Cookery sense plays an important part, too, just as we might say about card sense. I know an old fellow who has been playing casino for over 40 years. He never did play a good game—no card sense.

ZABAIONE.

Zabaione is a very delicious Italian dessert and is also known as Sabayon. The Italians serve it in a stemmed glass and, as it is a very light and foamy dessert, it is always eaten with a spoon. The French use it as a sauce for various puddings and cakes. The real Italian recipe calls for yolks only, but I like the French recipe better, as it calls for yolks and beaten whites.

Put eight egg yolks in large bowl and gradually beat in one cup of sugar until the mixture is light and frothy, then pour it into top part of double boiler. Do not have the hot water in the lower part of boiler touch the upper part, otherwise the egg yolks will cook instead of foaming.

Now add one-half cup of sweet sherry, gradually, and continue to beat until the Zabaione is very light and begins to thicken. Then remove it at once from upper part of double boiler and fold in the beaten whites until thoroughly blended. Serve in stemmed glasses while still warm.

January 28, 1938

The Rector restaurants of Chicago and New York specialized in shell fish and other sea food. Among those foods we went in for oysters in a big way. I mean by that, we conceived a great many ways of preparing the bivalve. Raw oysters on the half shell served with a cocktail sauce was probably the most popular.

Our oyster shipper in Virginia included in out weekly shipments one barrel of the largest Lvnnhavens that could be procured. They measured easily six inches from tip to tail, if any oyster has either. Lvnnhaven oysters contain oyster crabs, and among epicureans they were considered a delicacy eaten raw, right out of the oysters. Oyster crabs cooked a la Newburg or fried are the popular ways to do them in these days.

WHEN THE EDGES CURL UP
THEN OYSTER IS DONE

They used to say that cooked oysters were hard to digest. Well, that's all wrong. The only time you will have difficulty in digesting an oyster is when it is eaten raw and the beverage is whisky. Of course, there is such a thing as overcooking an oyster, so please remember that it is cooked when you see the edges curl and the body part is puffed up.

Bulk oysters, which are available in the food stores and sold by the quart or by the dozen, are, of course, fresh oysters carefully shipped in tubs packed in ice or in refrigerator cars.

One of the nicest ways to cook oysters is known as pan roast. This title is a misnomer, as they are cooked on top of the stove. It's a mighty tasty dish, to be sure. Purchase a dozen medium-sized oysters—they are usually poured into a carton with the oyster liquor. Put into a saucepan one tablespoon of butter; while it is melting add one-half teaspoon of paprika, one-eighth teaspoon of white pepper, and one-half teaspoon of celery salt.

To the melted butter add one dozen oysters and one third cup of oyster liquor. Bring to a boil and let boil another four or five minutes. Then add one third cup chili sauce, one half teaspoon Worcestershire sauce, and one-half cup cream. Stir gently, bring to boiling point, and serve on piece of freshly made toast. A soup plate is the ideal dish to serve a pan roast in.

Many years ago there was a famous oyster house in Philadelphia called Finelli's. Their specialty was oysters. I want you to try them prepared this way sometime. Here's how they are cooked. Those oysters are pan fried with butter:

PHILADELPHIA RECIPE FOR PAN FRIED OYSTERS.
Drain one dozen medium-sized oysters and season them with salt and pepper. Prepare a light batter as follows: One half cup of flour, one fourth teaspoon of salt, one teaspoon of baking powder, one-half cup of milk, and one egg. Mix and sift the dry ingredients, add milk gradually, and egg which has been well beaten.

Now mix three-quarters cup of finely chopped crab meat and three-quarters cup of bread crumbs. Dip oysters one at a time in the batter and then roll them in the crab meat and crumb mixture and then again in the batter, and once more in the crumb mixture. In a large skillet melt two or three tablespoons of butter and carefully lay the oysters in the pan. Cook them on one side until nicely browned and then turn them over with a spatula to cook and brown on the other side.

A very nice sauce to serve with these pan-fried oysters is tartare sauce. It's easy to make. To one-half cup of mayonnaise add one teaspoon each of finely chopped green peppers, pimientos, sweet pickles, and onions. Mix well and there you have a sauce which goes nicely with almost any fried shell fish or fried fish.

CREAMED OYSTERS.

I have another tasty oyster dish that we did in Rector's and that made a big hit. It is called creamed oysters. Here are the ingredients, and then I will give you directions how to cook them:

> Two small white onions, minced
> ½ cup of chopped mushrooms
> 2 tablespoons flour
> 2 tablespoons butter
> 1 cup cream
> ½ teaspoon salt
> few grains of cayenne pepper
> 1 dozen medium-sized oysters
> 1 tablespoon finely chopped parsley
> 2 tablespoons sherry.

Cook the onions and mushrooms a few minutes in butter or in the fat, which you prefer. Sprinkle in the flour and mix well. Add the cream and cook until it comes to a boil, stirring constantly. Now add the sherry, salt, and cayenne pepper. In another sauce pan cook the oysters in their own liquor. Do not overcook them. When you notice the edges curl up and the body part puff up, you will know they are cooked. Now add the oysters to the sauce, also the parsley. Stir well and serve in patty shells with an overflowing amount of sauce.

RECTOR TELLS HOW TO COOK CRABMEAT.

It took me a long time to become friendly with canned crabmeat. In my travels around the country I was more than surprised to see it served in so many fine restaurants and in well-managed homes, too. Last evening I opened a can and fixed up one of those hurry-up affairs when unexpected guests arrived. It's a good idea to have a few cans of crabmeat in the pantry. Well, this is what I did:

First I removed the bones—that's easy to do—and then I cut it in medium-sized pieces to make a cupful. Then I opened a can of condensed mushroom soup which I heated, but I did not dilute it. To the hot soup I added the crabmeat. I again opened a can of, this time it was pimientos. I was thinking, when I opened these cans, that you will regard me as one who lives from "can to mouth."

I chopped finely a tablespoon of pimientos and a tablespoon of green peppers; the latter I parboiled for a few minutes and added them to the crabmeat mixture and stirred well. A light pinch of cayenne pepper and one-half teaspoon of salt sufficed for the seasoning. When the mixture was thoroughly heated I added two tablespoons of dry sherry and stirred.

In using this recipe have prepared on one side a half dozen round pieces of toast about four inches in diameter. Spread the crabmeat mixture neatly on the toast, sprinkle with bread crumbs, dot with butter and brown in the oven or under the broiler flame. And there you have canape of crabmeat a la Rector.

February 4, 1938

It pleased me very much to receive so many letters in response for more salad combinations and salad dressings. I have always contended that the salad is almost as important as the main course of a meal. It should be served as a course. One of my favorite meals starts with a goodly quantity of soup—let's say onion soup—with oodles of grated cheese sprinkled over it and the piece de resistance—a salad, right out of that wooden bowl, a beverage and dessert. Now, don't you think that comes pretty near rounding out a nice meal? Of course, if you have a Rocky Mountain appetite this meal wouldn't go very far.

Sometime when you are going to prepare a shell fish salad—lobster, crabmeat, or shrimp, which usually calls for mayonnaise dressing—add to the dressing one-half teaspoon of curry powder and mix well. You will be surprised what a delicious flavor it has. Now here's another combination that originated in old Delmonico's—Lorenzo dressing. It is made by adding two tablespoons of chili sauce to one-half cup of French dressing, then add one teaspoon of finely chopped pimentos, one teaspoon of finely chopped chives, and one teaspoon finely chopped parsley, and mix well.

ON GLORIFYING SHREDDED CABBAGE.

You really can glorify shredded cabbage when you mix it well with sour cream dressing. Be sure and get the thick oozing kind of sour cream. To three-quarters cup of sour cream add one-quarter cup of vinegar slowly, stirring all the time. Season with one-half teaspoon of salt, a very light pinch of cayenne pepper, one-half teaspoon paprika, and one teaspoon of chives or finely chopped onion, preferably chives, all to be mixed well. Shred very finely a small solid head of white cabbage. Mix it well in the dressing and it wouldn't be a bad idea to put it in the refrigerator to chill. I have tried this very same dressing for a fruit salad, but I omitted the chives and added a teaspoon of powdered sugar.

Did you ever try a hot slaw? It's good, really it is. Shred finely three cups of cabbage and then start on the dressing. Mix together two tablespoons flour, two tablespoons sugar, one-half teaspoon salt, and one-half teaspoon of dry mustard. Add to dry ingredients two egg yolks which have been beaten with one-fourth cup of vinegar and three-quarters cup of rich milk. Cook in top part of double boiler, stirring gently until it thickens. When the dressing is cooked and perfectly smooth, add, and beat in well, two tablespoons of melted butter. Now add the shredded cabbage so that it will heat in the sauce without boiling.

When you fancy a potato salad and want one that is a little different try this:

Boil one half dozen medium-sized potatoes until tender, with their jackets on. Remove the jackets and drop the potatoes in a bowl. Break up the potatoes with two forks, but do not mash them. While the potatoes are still warm, pour over them one-third cup of French dressing, and let them marinate. Add one-half cup of finely sliced almonds, which have been previously blanched and skins removed. Also add one tablespoon of finely chopped onions and the same amount of finely chopped green peppers. Mix well. Now place the salad in refrigerator to chill. Just before serving add three-quarters cup of mayonnaise dressing and one tablespoon of finely chopped parsley. You will have to do some thorough mixing again and then serve this salad on a light bed of lettuce. A couple of dashes of paprika over the top will add a little color and flavor, too. The dressing which I gave you for the hot slaw would go very well in place of the mayonnaise.

USING LEFTOVER BOILED BEEF IN MEAT SALAD. Sometime when you are serving boiled beef or a pot roast and you find there is quite a bit left over for the next day, I want you to make a meat salad. It's delicious. Cut the meat in slices of one-quarter inch and then cut the slices in irregular pieces about the size of a half dollar. Go back to the refrigerator and see if you have any leftover, cooked vegetables. Perhaps you will find some beets, potatoes, or beans, string or limas. If so, you have the makings of a real salad.

Let us cut enough meat to make two cupfuls, which we will place in a bowl. Now cut the cooked vegetables in pieces as you have cut the meat, except, of course, the lima beans, which go in whole. One cupful of vegetables is enough. Add them to the meat and toss in one thinly sliced onion and one tablespoon of finely chopped parsley. To this combination add one-half cup of French dressing and do plenty of mixing. Serve on bed of lettuce garnished with hard cooked, sliced eggs.

I am very fond of leftovers—cold lamb, beef, chicken or veal—especially when prepared as a hash. I am going to do a whole column soon on various ways to prepare hash, and the title of it will be "Sweep Up the Kitchen."

February 11, 1938

When I was a small boy I was discovered up in an apple tree by the farmer. He wanted to know what I was doing up there. told him I was there for research purposes because I was studying botany. I soon found out that he didn't believe me, because I got a good seat warming from the leather strap he had in his hand. Today I offer no alibis in making the rounds of restaurants. I'm fond of good food and if I run across some new dish or sauce or salad, I'm going to pass it on to you. At that, there is nothing really new in the culinary art.

Once in a while I read some exotic food that calls for a cherry or two, with some chopped nuts and whipped cream. Well, that's all right if you like it. The chef of Simpson's, on the Strand in London, makes a steak and kidney pie exactly the same as he did many years ago. No one can improve on the Hungarian goulash that the late Mme. Sacher served in her famous restaurant in Vienna, and I might also include a certain meat loaf that I always rave about. It was home cooked and, oh, what a dish.

Those several dishes that I have mentioned, you will note, call for inexpensive cuts of meats. Slow cooking and plenty of basting are the secret for the tenderness and flavor. Over in Europe I have seen meats in the public markets that are almost as black as this type and I was amazed at the way this meat was cooked for tenderness and flavor.

A steak and kidney pie can be made from leftovers, but I'd rather have you use the raw meat.

TELL BUTCHER TO CUT BEEF IN 1½-INCH CUBES.

Tell your butcher to cut one and one-half pounds of chuck or round of beef in cubes about one and one-half inches. Have him slice one-half pound of veal or lamb kidneys in edible size pieces. Fry out a little beef fat in a sauce pan and in that fat brown lightly one onion finely chopped. Now add the meat and kidneys and brown thoroughly. If you have a cup of good stock add that. If no stock, then use water. Season with a teaspoon of meat sauce, one teaspoon salt, one-fourth teaspoon pepper, a very light pinch of cayenne pepper. Stir the whole mixture well, cover the saucepan, and send it on the way to cook. Let it simmer slowly for about two hours. If the sauce is too thin, thicken it with a little flour mixed to a smooth paste with a little water. Steak and kidney pie should have a fairly good quantity of sauce. That's easy—add more stock or water when the meat is nice and tender. Transfer it to an earthen or glass oven-proof casserole. Let it cool.

Now for the pastry covering. Chop three-quarters cup of shortening coarsely into two cups of flour, one teaspoon of salt, and one-half teaspoon of baking powder which have been sifted together. Separate one egg and mix the yolk with one-quarter cup of water. Cut this into the flour mixture. Roll the pastry on a lightly floured board to about one-third inch thickness. Cover casserole with pastry and brush top with egg white. Bake in hot oven until nicely browned.

Hungarian goulash also calls for inexpensive cuts of meat. Again tell the butcher to cut the meat, top round or chuck, in cubes of one and one-half inches. Fry out a little beef fat and brown the pieces of meat. Season with a teaspoon of salt and a light pinch of cayenne pepper.

To the meat add 3 pints of good stock, 2 buttons of garlic finely chopped, and 1 bay leaf. Cover saucepan and let it simmer for 2 ½ hours. Stir occasionally.

ADD THREE PINTS OF GOOD STOCK TO THE MEAT.

About 1 hour before goulash is cooked, add to it 6 medium-sized potatoes—peeled, of course. Cream together 3 tablespoons of butter with 2 tablespoons of paprika and 3 tablespoons of flour with a little of the liquid from the goulash. Add this paste, not all at once, to the goulash for the purpose of thickening the sauce. Paprika is a necessary seasoning in goulash. Stir well and then add 1 cup of puree of tomato. Please remember that the sauce is important, so don't be too skimpy with it. Serve on large platter and garnish each end with cooked noodles.

Now we come to that home cooked meat loaf that is a favorite of mine. Again we have to conjure with inexpensive cuts of meats. If I keep on writing about these cheaper cuts I may be able to solve the high cost of dining. At any rate I will try to keep you within your budget. Let's call this dish meat loaf, Bourgeoise. Here is the list of ingredients:

One pound ground beef, ½ pound ground pork, 4 slices of bread (soaked in warm milk and drained), ½ pound ground veal, 1 onion finely chopped, 2 teaspoons salt, ¼ teaspoon pepper, light pinch of cayenne pepper, 2 eggs, 1 cup of chili sauce, 2 tablespoons butter, 1 cup meat stock.

Put the three meats, the bread, onion, seasoning, and beaten eggs in a large bowl. Mix and mix and then do some more mixing. I have never been able to do a good mixing job unless I used my hands. I think you will agree with me. Form the meat into a loaf about two inches thick. Place it carefully in a greased baking pan—but be sure to allow a space on all sides of the loaf. Cover the loaf with the chili sauce, dot with butter, and pour around the sides the stock. Bake in moderate oven for about 50 minutes and don't forget to baste every 15 minutes.

There's a dish fit for the kings—the few there are left. Oh, yes, here's something else about this dish—if you think there is going to be too much, do not be concerned; its good when served cold, the next day, with a little mayonnaise on the side.

While I am on this matter of inexpensive cuts of meat I am going to tell you next week about a food which to my way of thinking is one of the most delectable and the least expensive of any dish I have ever tasted. It calls for pennies, not dollars, and is accompanied with a sauce that you all will enjoy.

February 18, 1938

Last week I promised to tell you about several foods that call for pennies rather than dollars. One of these is pig's feet and the other is tripe. The pig's feet, that I want you to prepare some time soon are the fresh pig's feet—strictly fresh, and please do not confuse them with the pickled variety. It takes a long time to cook these raw pig's feet. They are simmered for three or four hours in a large saucepan filled with water.

Suppose we start with six feet. Let the water come to a boil first, then put in the feet and lower the heat. Into the pan or pot in which the feet are cooking add one onion studded with cloves, several bay leaves, a pinch of thyme, a few outer stalks of celery, a small bunch of leeks and a few carrots. These vegetables added to the water is known in French cooking as court bouillon. Cover the saucepan and let them cook ever so slowly. When the feet are cooked remove them from the saucepan and lay them out to cool. Each foot should be cut lengthwise with a sharp cleaver, which will naturally produce twelve pieces of the feet. Prepare on the side about two cups of buttered bread crumbs, and roll or pat the pieces in these crumbs.

SAUCE YOU MUST USE.

Now comes the sauce, which you must not fail to serve. It's called sauce diablé—deviled sauce to you. Please make careful note of this sauce, because it goes fine if you happen to do a barbecue. Broiled veal kidneys too, aren't hard to take with deviled sauce

Now let's get started on the sauce. Pour into a small saucepan three-quarters cup of tarragon vinegar. Add two buttons of garlic, one tablespoon of dry mustard, two bay leaves, one teaspoon salt, one-half dozen whole black peppers, one teaspoon of paprika. Reduce by boiling this quantity to one-half and strain. To the remaining liquid add one cup of tomato puree or thick tomato soup. Stir and heat. Dissolve in one-half cup of boiling water two teaspoons of extract of beef. Add to the sauce also a teaspoon of Worcestershire sauce, a pinch of cayenne pepper, and lastly a tablespoon of butter. Do not boil the sauce, just keep it hot and serve hot.

Dot the flat side of the breaded pig's feet with butter and brown on a rack under the broiler flame or oven. It would be well to place the rack in the baking pan, because a little basting would do no harm.

Now, there you have a dish that will bring compliments from all sides. You have my permission to take the little bones in your mouth and bite off the tender morsels of meat. I get so enthusiastic about this dish that I am going out right now and get some pig's feet.

ASKS SOME ONE TO COIN WORD IN PLACE OF TRIPE.

It's a funny thing, but almost every time I talk about tripe I get the big ha! ha!—and I have found out the reason. The name tripe does it. Won't someone please coin a word in place of tripe? I feel sure I can sell you on the idea that tripe is a delicacy, but the tripe must be the fresh honeycomb tripe, not the pickled. There are ever so many ways of preparing it, and please remember that it is to be cooked in salted water for hours, same as pig's feet, but without herbs or vegetables.

Fresh honeycomb tripe must be thoroughly washed in cold water, and then when you start it bring the water to a boil, add salt, and simmer it for four or five hours. Change the water several times. No matter how you want to prepare it, give it plenty of cooking for tenderness.

After it is cooked cut it in small strips, say ¼-inch wide and about 2 inches long. Now, all we have to do is to make a creole sauce. Cut enough tripe to make 4 cupfuls and then we will proceed with the sauce. Slice 1 green pepper, 2 medium-sized onions, ½ pound of fresh mushrooms. Cook these vegetables for a few minutes in 1 cup of good stock or canned consommé. When cooked add the pulp of a No. 2 can of tomatoes, 1 small can of tomato puree, and ½ cup of minced cooked ham. Stir well and simmer for 10 minutes. Season sauce with 1 teaspoon salt, ½ teaspoon pepper, a light pinch of cayenne pepper, ½ teaspoon of paprika, and 1 teaspoon of Worcestershire sauce. Add the tripe, heat and mix well in the sauce. Just before serving drop in a tablespoon of butter.

HOURS OF SIMMERING MAKES TRIPE TENDER. That's all—and now you can settle down and enjoy a glorious dish, Again, please let me remind you, that the only way you can make tripe tender is hours of simmering before it is added to the sauce.

February 25, 1938

The other day I stopped in at the Ritz-Carlton to find out about the chicken hash that I have often heard is so delicious. I made a beeline for the kitchen and immediately went into a huddle with M. Diat, the chef. We discussed lamb hash, chicken hash, even corned beef hash.

M. Diat makes a chicken hash that you would find no difficulty in preparing in your own kitchen. Only white meat is used, that's because it's ritzy. The chicken is always cut into small cubes. Never a food chopper for this dish.

HEAT TWO CUPFULS CHICKEN MEAT IN A CUP OF STOCK.

Now let us start with 2 cupfuls of chicken meat which is heated in a cupful of chicken stock. Let it reduce about ⅓, I mean the stock, and then add 1 cupful of rich cream sauce. Do not forget the seasonings—salt and white pepper. Now we must prepare a Mornay sauce to pour over this delicious chicken hash when it is put into an au gratin dish for oven heating and slight browning.

Mornay sauce is made by adding grated Parmesan and grated Swiss cheese and butter alternately to a very hot cream sauce. It's a good sauce to know about, because it can be used with fillets of fish and also with egg dishes such as stuffed hard-cooked eggs.

Now. let us prepare about 2 cupfuls of cream sauce. While it is very hot—puffing hot, add 2 tablespoons of butter in little bits, stirring all the while. Also add the two cheeses, 1 tablespoons of each, little by little, and don't stop stirring. The whole idea is to blend in smoothly the cheese and butter. Intense heat and the stirring will do the trick. Turn the chicken hash into a shallow au gratin dish—coat the entire surface with Mornay sauce and sprinkle grated Parmesan cheese over the top. Now put a border of freshly mashed hot potatoes around the edge of the dish. This is easily done by forcing the mashed potatoes through a pastry bag. Place in moderate oven until lightly browned and serve immediately.

Whenever I see a roast leg or shoulder of lamb being served, I begin to think what I would like to do with it the following day, providing it becomes a left-over. It's good business to cook more than you expect to have consumed because I am going to try to sell you on the idea that a wet lamb hash is a delicacy. It's a pet dish of mine week in and week out.

If you have a cupful of lamb gravy left over so much the better and if not I would suggest using some good stock. Here are the ingredients:

One-half cup diced raw potatoes
¼ cup chopped onions
¼ cup chopped green peppers
3 tablespoons chopped pimentos
2 cups cold lamb—¼-inch cubes
1 cup left-over gravy
½ cup tomato puree or sauce
½ teaspoon salt
¼ teaspoon pepper
¼ teaspoon paprika
1 teaspoon meat sauce

2 tablespoons butter
2 tablespoons grated cheese.

Blanch the potatoes, onions, and green peppers. Cut the potatoes the same size as the cubes of lamb. Combine the gravy and puree of tomato and heat. Strain the vegetable; and add them along with the meat to the sauce. Now add the seasonings and heat thoroughly for 15 to 20 minutes—do not even let it simmer. If the sauce is too thick, add a little stock. Now, stir in the two tablespoons of butter and transfer the hash to an ovenproof au gratin dish. Sprinkle the cheese over the top and brown it.

CORNED BEEF HASH A NOBLE DISH IF MADE THIS WAY.

Corned beef hash! Now, there's a noble dish, when properly prepared. I always send the corned beef through the food chopper. I use ⅓ corned beef, ⅓ chopped cooked potatoes, and ⅓ chopped raw onions, which reminds me of something else I do by using thirds—it's a cocktail.

For corned beef hash, I use red onions, Italian onions. Combine the beef, potatoes and onions and let the mixture steam in a little water. Of course, it should steam long enough to cook the onions. Corned beef hash should be well seasoned—more pepper than salt. After the water has steamed away, drop a little butter into the pan and let the hash brown by banking it to the end of the pan. Turn it onto a platter with the brown side up. Place a poached egg on top, if you want to.

March 11, 1938

I have received a number of letters requesting a recipe for Hollandaise sauce. One lady wrote she wanted a "fool proof" recipe for Hollandaise sauce. In these letters the ladies of the kitchen complain about the sauce separating. Well! I can't blame them for that because I have seen it happen scores of times in the best of restaurants. A fine, smooth, thick Hollandaise could be picked up by the waiter in the kitchen and by the time it arrived before the guest it had separated for no reason at all.

There are ever so many foods that call for Hollandaise sauce. Asparagus, fresh or canned, and broccoli. Never before have I seen such firm, heavy and green broccoli in the markets. Cauliflower, when ladled in half milk and water and served with Hollandaise, is always popular. Boiled fish such a halibut, cod and any number of fishes have more zest and flavor with Hollandaise on the side. What makes eggs Benedict?—Hollandaise, of course.

PRINCIPLE SAME REGARDLESS OF THE NUMBER OF EGGS.

It doesn't matter one bit whether you are going to make Hollandaise with forty or four eggs. The principle is identically the same. To make this "fool-proof" you must be mindful of gentle heat. If you can strike that happy medium of heat, your sauce is sure to be a success. The recipe which I am going to give you has never failed me and I have done it a hundred times or more.

Melt one-half cup of butter over boiling water in the top part of a double boiler. Now remember, this is the only time I am going to mention the word "boiling." Your butter should be hot, but not too hot. Do you follow me? Meanwhile beat four egg yolks until thick, smooth and lemon colored. I prefer brown eggs and I don't know why. Pour beaten egg yolks into the melted butter all at once, and with a wooden spoon start stirring slowly, evenly, but don't stop stirring. Look out for the water in the lower part of the boiler, and do not at any time let it come to a boil. The hot steam from the water is going to cook your Hollandaise, just please remember that. Lift the top part from the lower part, if you think the heat is too great, but don't stop stirring.

With the necessary amount of heat you will soon begin to notice the sauce thicken, which means the butter and egg yolks are slowly cooking together. Right now add the seasonings, one fourth teaspoon salt and a very light pinch of cayenne pepper. One tablespoon of lemon juice is added when the sauce becomes fairly thick, perhaps just thick enough to pour, Keep the sauce warm, not hot. You see there is nothing really difficult is making Hollandaise sauce. Treat this prima donna of sauces kindly and it's bound to come out right.

CRABMEAT POPULAR EVEN IN FISHING SECTIONS.

A few weeks ago I had something nice to say about canned crabmeat. It is a popular food, even in sections of the country where fresh crabmeat is obtainable. Crabmeat Newburg makes a hit with almost every one. It was one of the best sellers in Rector's, and even today it is just as popular in the swank hotels and restaurants. There are several ways to prepare it. I would like to give you my version of it, by preparing the sauce very much like Hollandaise, except you do not need the double boiler.

First thing we do is to open a small can of crabmeat, or to be exact, the equivalent of one pound. The crabmeat should be carefully picked over to remove the little bones. Melt three tablespoons of butter in a saucepan. Add the crabmeat and mix it well and gently. I want it to absorb the butter and to heat thoroughly. Season with one half teaspoon salt and a light pinch of cayenne pepper. Add three tablespoons of dry sherry and mix again. Now here comes the trick, so follow closely. Bank the crabmeat to one side of the sauce pan so as to make a space to prepare the Newburg sauce,

Now, on with the recipe. Pour into the open space in the sauce pan one half pint of cream. Let it heat, not boil, over a low flame. Beat well three egg yolks as you would do for the Hollandaise sauce and pour the eggs slowly into the heated cream, stirring all the time with a wooden spoon. Be very careful that there is not too much heat. Occasionally remove the sauce pan from the low heat but do not stop stirring. If the eggs should cook too fast, because of a little too much heat, you will very likely wind up with scrambled eggs. Low heat will do the trick and your sauce will thicken and become smooth. Combine crabmeat and sauce and there you have crabmeat Newburg prepared in one pan.

March 18, 1938

I would much rather start a dinner or luncheon with a good soup than a fruit cocktail. These fruit combinations have a place in the menu all right—but the idea of eating something sweet before you get down to business doesn't click with me. It reminds me too much of breakfast. Serve these fruits as a salad or dessert—that's where they belong.

CLAIMS ONION SOUP AS ONE OF HIS FAVORITES. One of my favorite soups is onion soup. Over in France it might well be known as the national soup, judging from standpoint of consumption. Many of the swank restaurants in Paris charge 40 cents for a plate of onion soup au gratin, yet I have paid no more than four cents for a bowl of onion soup at the big market known as Halle Central in Paris, and it was mighty good, too.

When making onion soup there are two "musts"—onions must be sliced very thin and the stock must be good. I have decided to have a goodly quantity of onion soup for my dinner tonight, and I am not going out to buy a whole lot of soup bones and vegetables to make a stock. I shall invest in two cans of consommé. This consommé can be diluted by adding water, that is, if it is a concentrated consommé. Heat two cans of consommé with a cupful of water. Slice thinly six medium-sized onions. Melt two tablespoons of butter in a large saucepan. Add the onions and cook them until they become almost brown. Don't burn them. If you stir the onions around they will cook more evenly. Add more butter to the onions if needed. Season with one-half teaspoon of salt, a light pinch of cayenne pepper, one-half teaspoon paprika, and one teaspoon of Worcestershire sauce.

Now add the stock and simmer for a few minutes. Transfer the soup to an earthen soup casserole or one of those glass heatproof casseroles. Slice crosswise and thinly two hard rolls and toast the pieces. Spread these small pieces right on top of the soup. Sprinkle liberally with grated Swiss cheese and place in oven or under broiler flame to brown. Now doesn't that sound good? And so inexpensive, too!

Within the last few years a new soup has made its appearance. It's a wealthy soup and is served only in the fashionable hotels and restaurants. The name of this soup is Vichyssoise and is served cold.

NEW SOUP MAKES APPEARANCE AT SMART HOTELS.

Cut en Julienne, which means in very fine strips about two inches long, the white part of four leeks. Also slice thinly one small onion. Melt one or two tablespoons of butter in a saucepan and brown lightly the leeks and onion, then add five medium-sized raw potatoes thinly sliced, along with one quart of light-colored stock. Chicken or veal stock will do. Season with one-half teaspoon salt and a light pinch of cayenne pepper. Simmer gently, with cover on, for about one-half hour. Strain the soup through a fine strainer and force through the strainer as much of the vegetable pulp as you can. To this add two cups of hot milk and two cups of hot cream and bring just to a boil.

Let the soup cool and add another cup of cream. Place in refrigerator until thoroughly chilled. Just before serving sprinkle over the top of each cup one-half teaspoon of finely chopped chives. You will quickly observe that this Vichyssoise is a very rich soup, even without that last cup of cream.

ONE DISH COMBINES TOMATO AND PEA SOUP, THINNED.

A very popular soup that we served in Rector's was a combination of tomato and pea soup, equal parts, thinned out a bit with consommé. It was garnished with very thin strips of carrots and leeks, previously cooked, also a teaspoon of cooked peas to each cup. We called it potage mongole. Another nice combination is one can of thick tomato soup and one can of consommé, heated and served in cups with a gob of whipped cream on top.

I could make a lot of work for you, but it would be well worth while. The name of this soup is Mulligatawny. It's another one of those soups that comes mighty near making a whole meal. It happens to contain quite a few ingredients, so follow closely:

¼ cup of chopped onion
¼ cup diced carrots
¼ cup diced celery
¼ cup diced green pepper
1 apple sliced
4 tablespoons flour
1 teaspoon curry powder
1 cup diced cooked chicken
2 cloves
1 light pinch of mace
Few sprigs of parsley

1 quart white stock
1 cup canned tomatoes (pulp)
1 teaspoon salt
⅓ teaspoon pepper

Cook the vegetables and apple in sufficient butter until lightly browned. Add flour and seasonings, stir and blend thoroughly. Now add the stock and tomatoes. Simmer for one hour and add, if necessary, more stock. Strain and rub through a fine sieve, then add the chicken meat, and heat.

If you fancy having corn chowder some time I wish you would try this recipe:

½ cup chopped salt pork
1 bay leaf
½ teaspoon salt
¼ teaspoon pepper
2 cups water
1 cup raw potatoes diced
2 cups water
3 tablespoons flour
2 cups milk
1 small can corn (whole kernel)

Cook pork until lightly browned. Add onions and cook two or three minutes. Add seasonings, potatoes, and water. Thicken with flour mixed to a paste with a little cold milk. Add the remaining milk and corn. Heat thoroughly and serve.

March 25, 1938

We are very fortunate to have in this world fresh vegetables practically the year around. And we have them in cans, too. Of course, the canned vegetables come to you already cooked, but at that we can, by adding a little something here and there, improve the flavor. Take canned corn, for example, preferably the whole kernel pack:

ADD CHOPPED GREEN PEPPER TO CAN OF CORN. Open a No. 2 can. Melt two tablespoons of butter in a saucepan and thoroughly heat the corn. Add to the corn two tablespoons of green pepper finely chopped and previously blanched. Also add two tablespoons of finely chopped pimientos and one and one-half cups of rich cream. Stir and heat thoroughly. Season with a little salt and a light pinch of cayenne pepper. There's your corn Mexicaine, and you don't have to wait for the green corn on the cob to come along.

"SOUBISE" MEANS DISH HAS
ONION LURKING IN IT.
When you pick up a menu and read "eggs florentine," that means spinach is present. If it says "veal cutlets a la vichy" you can look for carrots. Any dish that has the word "soubise" tacked on is a sure bet to contain onions. I wish

some radio announcer would offer an automobile for the best answer to "I like French fried onions because—." Perhaps you will like them, too, when prepared as follows:

After you have peeled the onions, slice them evenly one-quarter of an inch thick. Separate the slices in rings and then place them in a shallow pan with enough milk to cover the slices. Let these onion rings soak in the milk for one-half hour. This soaking process is going to lessen that sharp onion taste. Spanish onions are the proper ones to use, but be sure you cut them thin enough. In the meantime, have ready your cooking fat in a deep-frying pan, good and hot. Now drain off the milk from the onion rings and drop them in a paper bag containing flour. If you are going to slice six Spanish onions, a cupful of flour in the bag will be just about right. Shake the onion rings well so that they will be evenly coated with the flour.

Now drop the onion rings in the deep, hot fat, but not all at once. Cook them in batches of a third at a time. When they have cooked to a nice golden brown, remove them and place them on absorbent paper for a few minutes and season immediately with salt and pepper. They should be kept hot while the balance is being cooked, so just transfer them to a hot platter and set in a moderate oven until the whole operation is completed.

The next time you are going to serve carrots, let's prepare them a la vichy. Now here's a treat, even for those who may dislike carrots:

Scrape and soak in cold water eight medium-sized carrots; slice them thinly. I would suggest using one of those vegetable slicers. The carrots should be sliced crosswise, ever so thin—the thinner the better. Boll in water until the carrots are tender. Drain off the water. Melt three tablespoons of butter in large saucepan, add the carrots, season with a little salt, pepper, and one-half teaspoon of powdered sugar. Cook the carrots in the butter, stirring them often to avoid burning. The carrots will absorb the butter and become just slightly brown. Just before removing them from the pan add two tablespoons of very finely chopped parsley and mix gently so as not to break the tender slices of carrots.

HERE'S HOW YOU CAN COOK PEAS WITHOUT WATER.

It's a good stunt to cook peas without water. Did you ever try it? You will want a heavy aluminum saucepan and a heavy cover. Shell enough peas to make a cupful.

Put two tablespoons of butter in the saucepan. Soak several outer leaves of lettuce in cold water, but do not dry the leaves. It's the water which clings to the leaves that supplies the moisture in the cooking. Line the bottom of the pan with the leaves, with the butter under the leaves. Place the peas over the leaves. Season with salt and pepper to taste and sprinkle over the top one-half teaspoon of powdered sugar. Now place another layer of wet lettuce leaves on top of the peas and clamp on the heavy cover.

April 1, 1938

A few months ago, when I was out in Hollywood, I met a lot of old friends and among them was Adolphe Menjou. Aside from being a good actor Menjou can talk food and recipes like a master cordon bleu chef. He's an epicure, and is especially fond of the French cuisine. I fully agree with him on that. His father, you may know, was a famous French restaurateur. Menjou reminded me of one of our specialties in Rector's that he praised very highly. It was lobster a l'Americanne, and then we discussed ever so many dishes, various ways of preparing filet of sole, ragouts, and salads.

We got to talking about the restaurants in Paris, particularly of that delightful little restaurant on the Rue de l'Echelle, Cafe Montagne, where the proprietor, Prosper Montagne, is the chef.

Menjou raved about the way our friend Montagne prepared chicken, otherwise known as Poulet Maison. I remember the dish very well and this is the way he did it.

Cut a small chicken, weighing about two and one-half pounds, in six or eight pieces. Season with salt and pepper to taste. Melt two tablespoons of butter in a heavy saucepan. Lay the pieces of chicken in the very hot butter. Brown them on one side and then turn them to brown on the other side. Now place cover over saucepan and continue cooking in oven until chicken is tender. About 15 minutes before chicken is cooked, add one cupful of diced fresh mushrooms. Remove chicken from oven and add two tablespoons chopped truffles along with three tablespoons of cooking sherry. Let it come to a boil and then add one cup of cream and heat thoroughly. Arrange the pieces of chicken in a platter and pour this delicious sauce over the chicken.

I want you to know about the lobster a l'Americanne, that is an outstanding gastronomic delight. Such dishes as lobster Newburg, chicken a la king, shrimps creole are reheats, but when you cook lobster in the shell, you are most certainly going to get the essence of the lobster in the sauce. Now we will proceed with the recipe.

A female lobster is preferable because of the roe. Have the butcher cut the whole live lobster (weighing about two and one-half pounds) in crosswise sections in one and one-half inch pieces. Have the claws cut in halves. The lobster meat is not to be removed from the shell, but have the roe carefully removed. Put about six tablespoons of olive oil in a large saucepan and when the oil is very hot add the sections of lobster (in the shell), three tablespoons brandy, ignite the brandy and add one cup of fish consommé. (This is obtained by simmering one pound of inexpensive fish and fish bones along with a soup bunch until the essence is extracted.) Season with salt, pepper, and paprika. Cover pan and cook for 20 minutes, occasionally turning the pieces of lobster.

Meanwhile prepare the following: Two small carrots, chopped very fine, one clove of garlic, chopped fine, four medium-sized fresh or canned tomatoes, cut in quarters, and the roe of the lobster, chopped fine. Add chopped vegetables and roe to lobster along with a pinch of thyme, one small bay leaf and one cup of tomato sauce. Cook all together for 15 or 20 minutes.

April 8, 1938

I received a letter from an old friend of mine, who is now retired and living in Southern California. He wanted the recipe for Ragout of Beef a la Deutsch. This dish was named after a vivant by the name of William Deutsch, one of Delmonico's best cash customers. It's a dish which calls for the tip ends of the tenderloin of beef. We served it in Rector's, but we never got any culinary citation for it.

I wanted to know more about this famous Ragout a la Deutsch so I went over to Delmonico's one evening and ordered it. It was delicious!

Our chef tried very hard to match it, but some one little thing in the sauce was missing. We got it all right within a couple of weeks by hiring out of Delmonico's the sauce cook who made it. This chap was only 28 years old and two years later was appointed chef of Rector's, perhaps the youngest chef ever to have had charge of a kitchen in an important restaurant. So now, my dear readers, I will introduce to you the recipe for Ragout a la Deutsch.

SUBSTITUTE SLICED SIRLOIN FOR FILET ENDS. The tail ends of the large tenderloin taper down to a rather thin point, which could not he formed into a filet mignon, so every few days we were stocked up on these filet tips. Now I am not asking you to purchase these filet ends because they would be terribly expensive. You can, however, purchase about two pounds of sirloin and ask the butcher to slice it about one-quarter of an inch thick and then cut in irregular size pieces about the size of a half dollar.

Suppose we start with two cupfuls of this thinly sliced sirloin. Now melt in a saucepan three or four tablespoons of butter and when very hot toss in the meat and also one-half cup of lamb kidneys thinly sliced. Season with salt, and pepper. Brown and cook meat and kidneys quickly over hot fire. On the side have ready one-half cup of boiling water in which has been dissolved two teaspoons of extract of beef, pour this in the pan. Also add one-half cup of cooked potatoes thinly sliced and one-half cup of green peppers thinly sliced and previously blanched. Stir well and let simmer for about five minutes and then finish it with one tablespoon of butter.

Ragout a la Deutsch is not exactly a stew, so there should not be too much sauce, nor should the sauce be too thin. You are going to like this ragout very much and I am sure you will serve it often in your home.

NEW ENGLAND VERSION OF BAKED BEANS.

A few years ago I wrote into one of my articles for the *Saturday Evening Post* a recipe for Boston baked beans. I thought it was a good recipe, until a lady up New England way wrote me her version of baked beans. I cooked them and they were the best I ever tasted. May I pass this recipe on to you? This is the lady's title for Boston baked beans, "1,001st Recipe for Baked Beans." The only good one!

Cover 2 cups of pea beans with 4 cups cold water and place in a cool place to soak overnight. In the morning, if the beans have not absorbed all the water, drain it off and save it, although this proportion is just about right for complete absorption of the water. Start the beans to cook with fresh cold water to cover, about 3½ cups, and cook over low flame in a tightly covered saucepan.

Beans must not boil, so remember to keep the flame low and the saucepan tightly covered while they are simmering. By doing this our process becomes one of steaming and the beans will swell and gradually absorb some of the water. One hour of simmering (from the time the simmering point is reached) is ample time to prepare the beans for the bean pot and oven cooking.

Carefully drain the beans, saving the water. Place a slice of salt pork on the bottom of the earthen pot and pour in the beans. Now bury a piece of scored salt pork weighing about ½ pound in the center of the beans and prepare the seasoning as follows:

One-half cup of Puerto Rico molasses mixed with ½ cup of bean water or plain boiling water, ½ teaspoon of mustard, ¼ teaspoon of paprika and 1 scant teaspoon of finely chopped onion. Mix thoroughly and pour over beans, lifting the beans carefully with a spoon so the seasoning will go to the bottom of the bean pot. Cover the bean pot and place in a slow oven for 6 hours.

Once an hour add a little water, lifting the beans gently so the water will go through. The water should be about even with the beans. If too much water the beans will be stewed, if too little, they will dry.

Uncover the bean pot the last hour of cooking so the pork may become crisp and browned. Serve with Boston brown bread. A real treat.

April 15, 1938

Hors d'oeuvres is hard to pronounce and would trip many a crack speller in a spelling contest. The word or words are French, of course, meaning in our language, appetizers. In Sweden they are called smorgasbord. In the old days, before they plastered signs in front of places reading "cocktail bar" it was "saloon" and instead of hors d'oeuvres they had free lunch.

Serving hors d'oeuvres today is more popular than ever. I have noticed in the food stores they have many ready to fill puff paste miniature croustades that come in boxes, and you will also find a number of various pastes that are already prepared that come in tubes, such as anchovy paste, shrimp paste, etc.

HERE'S A NICE COMBINATION.

In Rector's we had perhaps 20 to 30 different hors d'oeuvres and I shall be pleased to pass on to you the recipes for some of these tasty snacks. Now here's a nice combination. You can serve it on small rounds of toast, cut an inch and one-half in diameter, or in some of those prepared puff paste creations that can be purchased in the stores.

To 1 small package of cream cheese, add 3 tablespoons of grated carrots and 1 tablespoon of horseradish, but be sure to squeeze out the vinegar or preferably use the freshly grated horseradish. Now moisten and mix thoroughly with 1 tablespoon of mayonnaise. Season with a few grains of cayenne pepper and a light pinch of salt. When the mixture is perfectly smooth, place it in a pastry bag and force it through onto the small rounds of toast.

Deviled stuffed eggs are popular, too, and they are also easy to prepare. Remove the yolks from 6 hard cooked eggs which have been cut lengthwise, cream the yolks with 1 tablespoon of anchovy paste, ½ teaspoon of Worcestershire sauce and 2 or 3 tablespoons of mayonnaise. Season only with a light pinch of cayenne pepper. When this mixture has been creamed to a smooth paste, place in a pastry bag and fill up the egg whites. Decorate the top of each egg piece with several capers.

GOOD TO SERVE WITH SALAD COURSE.

Cheese puffs are tasty and simple to prepare. Mix together ¼ cup of soft white bread crumbs, ½ teaspoon paprika, a little salt and a light pinch of cayenne pepper. Separate 1 egg and to the yolk add 1 teaspoon of Worcestershire sauce and beat until mixed. Then add it to the seasoned bread crumb mixture. Now add 1 cupful of grated American cheese and fold in the egg white stiffly beaten. Mix all these ingredients thoroughly and form in small balls. This quantity will make about 10 balls. Roll these small balls in fine dry bread crumbs and fry in deep fat until they take on a nice golden brown. Drain on absorbent paper. Insert a wooden pick in each of these cheese balls and there you are! Cheese puffs are also delicious to serve with the salad course.

The other day I received a letter from a friend of mine in London who raved about a little snack that he had in Boulestin's restaurant. It's called anchoiade and naturally calls for anchovies. Chop fine 2 dozen medium-sized anchovies, ¼ cup of chopped walnuts, 1 tablespoon of finely chopped parsley and one small button of garlic grated. Moisten with a tablespoon of olive oil and mix thoroughly. Now spread this mixture on small rounds of buttered toast. This combination goes well as a sandwich spread, and remember, picnic days are not far away.

SHRIMPS IN A SPECIAL SAUCE.

What is more delicious than a bowl of fresh shrimps served with a special sauce? To be sure the shrimps are boiled in salted water. Remove the shells and also the little black streak running down the back of 2 pounds of shrimps. Now for the sauce. To 1 cup of mayonnaise, add the following finely chopped: One tablespoon of stuffed olives, 1 tablespoon of green peppers, 1 teaspoon of chives and 1 teaspoon of lemon juice. Mix the shrimps in this sauce.

Many of the old gourmets that patronized Rector's used to combine Roquefort cheese and cream cheese. Force through a sieve ¼-pound of Roquefort cheese and to it add 1 small package of cream cheese, 1 tablespoon horseradish, from which squeeze out the vinegar, 1 teaspoon of paprika, 1 teaspoon of Worcestershire sauce and 4 tablespoons of dry sherry. Cream together the two cheeses and mix in well the other ingredients.

This cheese mixture can be spread on potato chips, on crackers or on small rounds of toast. I think you will find it more appetizing to the eye if the mixture is put in a pastry bag and forced through in a decorative way on small thin rounds of toast.

April 22, 1938

The other day a letter came from a gentleman which brought up pleasant memories. I got quite a kick reading it so I thought it would be a good idea to let my readers in on it, too.

> "Dear Sir: In the middle of the '80s, I often had minced clams on toast at Charles Rector's (my father), where I was greeted with his smiles, though we never met. About two years ago I found the dish on the menu at the Hotel — and felt glad at the prospect of having this dish again. It came. The clams were minced and the bread was toasted and that was all. The brown sauce of Rector's was missing. If this dish is in a book by you, please let me know and I shall order a copy.
> "Yours very truly,
> "J. J. Kerrigan, M. D., Michigan City, Ind."

Dear Doctor: Now let's see—the middle '80s—my goodness, that goes back a little over half a century and that's a long time to remember a certain dish that you enjoyed in my father's restaurant! The recipe which I am going to give you is before me now. It appeared in a little booklet with ever so many of my father's specialties. This little booklet was published just about 50 years ago and was given to our patrons as a souvenir.

MINCED CLAMS ON TOAST, CHARLES RECTOR STYLE.

"Open two dozen little neck clams and chop tolerably fine, using care to save all the liquor. Put into a pan with half an ounce of butter and season with red pepper and Worcestershire sauce. Stew for a few minutes and thicken with cream sauce. Serve on toast."

This recipe is too brief and I think it best to explain it more clearly. The clam juice or liquor should be used right down to the last drop. While the clams are cooking put a cover on the pan. The cream sauce is rich, it is made with cream and not milk. A little more than a cupful of cream sauce is sufficient. The sauce should be the right consistency, not too thick nor too thin. A tablespoon of Worcestershire and the clam juice mixed in with the cream will produce a sort of brownish sauce. The toast is freshly made and that's always important.

And there you are, Doctor. I've not only tried to describe this delicacy, "blow by blow," but have just finished cooking and eating minced clams on toast myself. It's a swell dish. I hope we will both be enjoying the clams 50 years from now.

SAUCE FOR COLD CUTS OF GAME.

Simpson's, that famous restaurant on the Strand in London, serves with cold cuts or game a sauce that I will never forget. The chef's name was Wille, a big, fine-looking Englishman, who prepared the sauce before me out in the kitchen. Here are the ingredients. It is called the Cumberland sauce:

3 tablespoons red currant jelly
3 tablespoons port wine
2 tablespoons orange juice
1 tablespoon lemon juice
1 teaspoon mixed English mustard
1 teaspoon paprika
½ teaspoon ground ginger
3 tablespoons of orange rind, finely shredded

Melt the jelly over a low fire until liquid and let it cool. Now add the port wine, orange juice, lemon juice, mustard, paprika, ground ginger and the orange rind. Mix well. Before adding the very thinly sliced orange rind, blanch it in boiling water for a few minutes and drain. By the way, before you cut the rind remove the white part. This sauce should be served not exactly cold—let's say room temperature. Bring on the cold cuts, James!

I have already given you in this column a standard recipe for French dressing; now comes one for mayonnaise:

4 egg yolks
3 cups olive oil
¾ cup vinegar
1 teaspoon salt
⅛ teaspoon cayenne pepper
1 teaspoon dry mustard.

Put into a fairly large chilled bowl four egg yolks, add the seasonings and mix well. Now the rest of the procedure is one of mixing, beating, and more mixing, by first adding slowly a little oil, then a little vinegar, and so on until the oil and vinegar are all used.

Did you ever try horseradish in mayonnaise? It's wonderful. Just add one tablespoon of freshly grated horseradish to one-half cup of mayonnaise. Mix well and then fold in one-half cup of whipped cream. This goes well with a meat salad.

Mayonnaise Figaro is another delicious combination. All you have to do is chop finely one tablespoon of chives and add them to one-half cup of mayonnaise, along with two tablespoons of tomato sauce, and mix well.

April 29, 1938

When William Makepeace Thackeray stopped off at New Orleans, he overstayed his visit for one very good reason—it was the food. New Orleans cooking is very definitely of the French type, but is generally called creole cooking.

A FISH AND SHELLFISH STEW.

Mr. Thackeray had a lot of nice things to say about a certain dish known as lobster bouillabaisse. The dish did not originate in New Orleans, it made its debut in or about Marseilles. France. Bouillabaisse is a fish and shellfish stew. It's not so difficult to prepare, but it does contain ever so many ingredients, particularly herbs and spices.

Now for the recipe for Bouillabaisse Marseillaise:

3 pounds fish
3 pounds shellfish
1 quart fish stock
½ cup olive oil
1 tablespoon finely chopped onion
1 tablespoon finely chopped celery
1 tablespoon finely chopped parsley
1 teaspoon finely chopped garlic
1 teaspoon finely chopped sage
1 teaspoon finely chopped thyme

1 teaspoon saffron leaves
6 tomatoes chopped, 1 teaspoon salt
⅓ teaspoon cayenne pepper
1 teaspoon paprika
1 cup dry white wine (sauterne)

Use fresh, firm salt water fish and filet them. Make a good stock from the carcasses, head and tail. Pour the oil into a large flat sauce pan. When the oil is hot put in the fish and shellfish. For the shellfish use live lobster, split lengthwise, shrimp and crabmeat. The lobster must remain in shell. Blanch the shrimp and remove shells. Add all the seasonings (herbs and spices) except the parsley. Stir around gently. All of this preliminary cooking should take not more than 10 minutes. Now add the fish stock and white wine, cover the saucepan and cook for 30 minutes. Sprinkle over the top the finely chopped parsley and serve in soup plates.

BETTER TASTING DRESSING THAN MAYONNAISE. Last week I gave a recipe for standard French mayonnaise. In the meantime I ran across a salad dressing on the order of mayonnaise, but better tasting by far, I think. It calls for olive oil or the salad oil which you prefer.

¾ cup oil
1 tablespoon sugar
2 teaspoons dry mustard
1 teaspoon salt
⅛ cayenne pepper
2 egg yolks
¼ cup vinegar
2 tablespoons corn starch

Pour oil in a mixing bowl. Mix and sift sugar, mustard, salt and cayenne. This is important, as dry mustard is usually lumpy and this thorough sifting will prepare it for smooth amalgamation with balance of ingredients. Add sifted seasonings to oil, also add the egg yolks and vinegar, but do not stir. Add one-half cup of cold water to the cornstarch and smooth. Now add another one-half cup of cold water and cook over low heat, stirring constantly until boiling point is reached and mixture becomes clear. Remove from heat and continue stirring for about three minutes. Pour hot cornstarch mixture on top of ingredients in mixing bowl and beat briskly with rotary egg beater until it's smooth and creamy like. Chill in refrigerator before serving.

This salad dressing should be the same thickness as regular mayonnaise and in appearance they are exactly alike. Try this dressing on potato salad some time and it goes wonderfully well on meat or fish salads and cold asparagus. Cooked vegetable salad mixed with this dressing will surely make a hit. Oh, yes, just one more suggestion, the next time you serve avocados, drop into each half a tablespoon of it.

May 6, 1938

The serving of aperitifs is more popular today than ever. Cocktails which come under that heading are really an old American custom. In Rector's we had such fastidious patrons that a few drops more or less of gin or Vermouth in their cocktails would be detected. Perhaps you might be interested in knowing a formula for making a perfect Martini cocktail. Here it is and with best wishes:

FORMULA FOR PERFECT MARTINI COCKTAIL. Measure out the gin and Vermouth with great accuracy, as this is the only way to get a perfect tasting cocktail. Also, only make the quantity that is to be served. If a second cocktail is served then you must start all over again to measure out the ingredients. Since a Martini cocktail stirred and never frapped, the ideal receptacle for mixing is a pitcher or cocktail bucket which has a spout for pouring.

Now the first procedure is to get the cocktail glasses thoroughly chilled and into each glass pour three or four drops of Grand Marnier. (This is a liqueur with a delightful orange flavor.) Twirl the glasses until they are coated with the liqueur. Now for the mixing. A perfect Martini is made by measuring sixths—so we will take four-sixths dry gin, one-sixth Italian Vermouth and one-sixth French

Vermouth. Put the gin and Vermouth into the pitcher with large cubes of ice and with a long handled spoon stir until the cocktail is thoroughly chilled. Pour into the glasses you have prepared and squeeze a small piece of lemon rind over the top of each cocktail to impart the zest of the lemon. Do not drop the lemon rind into the cocktail, but if you do relish a tid-bit of some sort in your Martini, drop in a well-drained pitless olive or a tiny white pickled onion, also well drained.

COFFEE SERVED WITH A DASH OF SHOWMANSHIP.

When you are having guests and would like to serve coffee with a dash of showmanship then proceed with "Cafe Diablé." Make a quantity of strong coffee, enough for eight or 10 small cups, and keep the coffee hot. Put in a chafing dish that has direct heat two sticks of cinnamon, one teaspoon of whole cloves, one teaspoon of coriander seeds, eight or 10 lumps of sugar, one tablespoon of whole coffee beans, a small piece of lemon and orange rind. Let these spices get thoroughly heated and then add about four tablespoons of brandy.

When the brandy has become thoroughly heated, ignite it from the flame of a match. Spoon or ladle constantly while the brandy is burning. When the flame has died out, pour in the hot black coffee and one tablespoon of Curacao. (Curacao is a liqueur, also delightful, with a decided orange flavor). Now pour into the ladle four tablespoons of brandy and drop in three or four lumps of sugar and again ignite and let sugar and brandy brown in the ladle until sugar is melted and brandy is burned out. Ladle all together and serve in after-dinner coffee cups. During all this preparation the heat must be under the chafing dish from start to finish.

SIMPLE BUT SWANK DESSERT.

For a simple but rather swank dessert I am offering you a maple parfait:

To ¼ cup of maple sirup add 1 tablespoon of butter. Stir over low heat and let boil one minute. Beat 2 egg yolks in top part of double boiler and gradually add the hot maple sirup. Continue beating and cook over hot water until very light and fluffy. Then fold the mixture into 2 stiffly beaten egg whites. Set in refrigerator to chill.

Meanwhile beat ½ pint of cream until stiff, add a few grains of salt and 1 teaspoon of vanilla extract. Beat egg mixture into whipped cream and freeze in chilling unit for 3 hours.

Serve in parfait glasses and decorate each parfait with bits of candied fruit. Arrange to form a design. For instance, cut a candied cherry into eight parts and arrange the pieces in daisy design. Fill in the center with finely chopped green gage or angelica. Or, if you prefer, sprinkle finely chopped walnuts on top of parfait.

May 13, 1938

There is a wealth of service being rendered to the housewife in the matter of cookery. Newspapers, magazines, radio, utility companies, and national food manufacturers are doing their utmost to bring good cookery in the homes.

I am very happy to report that the ladies of the kitchen are taking advantage of this fine service. Interest in the culinary art is greater than ever, and as a result, we can boast of having, in this land of ours, I think, the best cooks in the world.

Kitchens today are made so attractive that it is a pleasure to work in them. I remember way back, when dilapidated bric-a-brac, broken chairs and what not were relegated to the kitchen. These up-to-date kitchens are equipped with ever so many labor-saving gadgets, modern refrigerators, kitchen cabinets and good-looking ranges, both gas and electric, makes a mighty fine stage setting not only for the preparation of the meals, but offers a most inviting place for a small family to eat their meals.

FINE RECIPE FOR LAMB KIDNEY STEW.
If you fancy a lamb kidney stew some time I have a splendid recipe to offer you. Here are the ingredients:

Six lamb kidneys, ½ cup sliced fresh mushrooms, 1 tablespoon chopped onions, 3 tablespoons butter, 2 tablespoons flour, 1 cup bouillon, ½ teaspoon salt, ⅛ teaspoon cayenne pepper, 1 green pepper sliced, 2 tablespoons sherry.

Wash kidneys, remove skin and cut into quarter inch slices. Cook kidneys, mushrooms and onions in butter a few minutes over hot fire. Add flour and stir until well blended. Add bouillon, green pepper, salt, and pepper and cook over low heat for about 15 minutes. Just before serving add the sherry. The bouillon I refer to can be purchased in cans. You could use, if you prefer, a tablespoon of extract of beef dissolved in a cup of boiling water.

In ever so many of these stews and ragouts, I believe the sauce is quite as important as the dish itself. In order to get that real flavor in the sauce, a good stock must be used and that is why I am forever recommending the use of extract of beef or the bouillon.

SPOON BREAD AS MAMMY MAKES IT.

It takes a real Southern mammy to make spoon bread. When I found the twain I decided I wanted to know all about it, so I asked mammy if she would make another batch of it in my presence and she did. It was perfect! Now if you will follow this recipe very closely, you will have as a result the best spoon bread that ever came out of the South.

Two cups of boiling water, 1 cup of yellow corn meal, 1 tablespoon of butter and 1 ½ teaspoons of salt. Cook the above ingredients in top part of double boiler for several minutes, stirring until mixture is thick. Then pour mixture into large bowl to cool. Separate 4 eggs. Reserve the whites. They are to be used later. Beat egg yolks with ½ cup of milk, using a rotary beater. Add to the cool corn meal mixture and do some more beating. Now sift together ½ cup of flour, 2 tablespoons of sugar and 2 tablespoons of baking powder and add to the corn meal mixture and mix thoroughly. Beat the egg whites to a stiff froth and fold them into the mixture.

Now for the baking. Pour mixture into buttered baking dish, a dish with a depth of about four inches, but do not fill the dish—just pour in enough to half fill the baking dish, because the mixture is going to rise just about double. Bake in moderate oven for 30 to 35 minutes, and there you have spoon bread par excellence. Serve at table from dish spoon bread was baked in.

RECIPE FOR THE FAMED YORKSHIRE PUDDING.

A recipe for Yorkshire pudding would fit in here very nicely. A fine rib roast is hardly complete without the famed Yorkshire pudding to accompany it.

Three-quarter cup flour, ¼ teaspoon salt, ½ pint milk, 2 eggs (well beaten).

Sift flour and salt into mixing bowl. Make a well in the center and gradually add enough milk to make a paste about the consistency of heavy cream. Now add the eggs (they should be beaten with a rotary egg beater for five minutes) to the remainder of the milk and with a large wooden spoon beat the egg and milk mixture into the flour and milk mixture.

Please remember we have two mixtures, so do not let that confuse you. All right, now beat well until large bubbles rise to the surface. Let mixture stand for almost an hour, then pour it into a shallow baking pan containing one-quarter inch of hot roast beef fat. A baking pan measuring about 10 by 10 inches is the perfect size. The mixture in pan should he just a little over one-half inch high. Bake in hot oven (400 degrees) for 20 minutes, then decrease heat to moderate and bake 10 minutes longer. Cut the pudding in squares and with a good spoonful of the roast-beef juice.

GINGERSNAP GRAVY FOR POT ROAST.

A pot roast on a dinner table is always welcome, and for those who like to do a little sopping now and then, there's a delicious sauce that goes with this pot roast and the sauce is called gingersnap gravy.

Make a marinade as follows: Two cups of vinegar, 2 cups of water, 2 bay leaves, 6 whole black peppers, 1 onion (sliced), a pinch of mace and 3 or 4 cloves. Bring vinegar, water and the spices to boiling. Remove from fire and cool. Pour the marinade over a 4- or 5-pound piece of pot roast and let stand in the refrigerator for 2 days, turning it several times so it will pickle evenly. Remove the meat from the marinade and wipe it dry on all sides. Dredge with flour and sear on all sides in hot fat in a heavy pot-roast kettle. Now add one cup of the marinade, season with salt, cover the kettle and cook over low heat about three hours or until meat is very tender. While the meat is cooking, turn it and baste occasionally.

Remove the pot roast to a hot platter and make the gravy as follows: Mix 3 tablespoons of flour to a smooth paste with cold water and stir it into the liquid in the pot-roast kettle. If there is not sufficient liquid in the kettle, then add a cupful or so of the marinade. You will want two cupfuls of gravy. Bring this gravy to the boiling point and let it boil for several minutes. Strain into hot gravy bowl and add cup of finely rolled gingersnap crumbs.

May 20, 1938

It was almost unheard of for a restaurant in the old days of Delmonico's and Rector's to do any advertising. We went on the theory of mouth-to-mouth advertising. It was old-fashioned, that I will admit, but we prospered just the same.

On the other hand, we searched Europe to procure souvenirs to present to the ladies, such as fans and vanity cases. The Parisian restaurants, I found, were the pioneers in the matter of souvenirs. It was my business to make an annual trip to Paris, not only to dig up new dishes, but to get a line on what would please the ladies.

We never bothered much about presenting anything to the gentlemen, except the check at the end of the meal. Ash trays showing the exterior of Rector's were very popular. We purchased many thousands of them, but didn't get much of a chance to give them away. Our customers took it for granted that the trays belonged to them, so they just put them in their pockets.

I don't know how many pullman towels are taken during the year, but on a pro rata basis, we could show an equal loss in silver demitasse spoons, cups and saucers.

FRUIT SAUCE FOR BRAISED DUCKLING.
Braised Long Island duckling with macedoine of fruits, served with a marmalade sauce, might well be called a

piece de resistance. Have the butcher cut a duckling in eight pieces. Season with salt and pepper. Brown the pieces on both sides in hot butter in a large skillet. Add to the duckling one cup of consommé. Place skillet, covered, in oven and cook for one hour or until the duckling is tender. Cut in very thin strips the rind of one orange (do not cut any of the white pulp with the rind) and blanch these strips for a few minutes. Place the pieces of duckling on a hot platter on top of the oven to keep hot. Skim off the fat from the liquid remaining in the skillet and add the juice from the orange, the blanched orange rind strips and one tablespoon of marmalade. Heat and stir thoroughly. Pour this sauce over the duckling and garnish with small bouquets of hot diced fruits, such as pears, peaches, pineapple, and grapes. If fresh fruits are used, then stew these fruits in water and sugar.

STUFFED LAMB MELTS IN THE MOUTH.

If you want to cook a certain cut of lamp that just about melts in your mouth try a forequarter of lamb, but ask the butcher to trim and bone the shoulder for stuffing. Now the first procedure is to prepare the stuffing, and that is done as follows:

Six cups of soft breadcrumbs, ⅓ cup of melted butter or any shortening you prefer, 1 teaspoon of salt, ½ teaspoon of thyme, 1 tablespoon of finely chopped celery, 1 tablespoon of finely chopped parsley, and 1 cup of chopped mushrooms. Mix well by tossing lightly with a large spoon. Stuff the lamb and sew it up.

Place lamb in roasting pan and then in a very hot oven for 20 minutes. Baste and turn the lamb so that it will brown nicely. Reduce the heat and continue cooking, allowing 20 minutes to the pound. Season with salt and pepper, and, if you like garlic, puncture the lamb in a few places and insert a thin strip of garlic, that to be done at the very start.

When the lamb is cooked, place on hot platter. Pour off all but three tablespoons of the liquid in roasting pan and thicken with two tablespoons flour. Now add one cup of good stock or water and one-half cup of tomato sauce. Cook this sauce on top of stove, stir well so as to loosen up any of the essence of the meat which clings to the pan.

Again I must repeat, for real tenderness and for real good eating, these inexpensive cuts of meats cannot be surpassed. Please remember the secret is in the slow cooking and basting.

May 27, 1938

An experienced or practical cook naturally will have less difficulty following a recipe than one who is just learning. During my time I have read thousands of recipes, a great many good ones and some poor ones.

If you have a failure in preparing a certain dish or sauce, do not put the blame entirely on the recipe itself, unless of course, the recipe is written in such a way as to be confusing.

Only a few weeks ago, I wrote in this column a recipe for Hollandaise sauce.

As I recall, it took about half the column to give it. The recipe was a success all right because I received a great many letters from readers who took the trouble to write me that at long last they have mastered Hollandaise. Mrs. C. D. wrote as follows:

"I want to thank you for the articles and recipes, which I find very helpful. For instance, I had been making Hollandaise sauce for years, and occasionally I had a failure which I could not explain. In a recent issue you explained why that failure occurred. I think countless wives and even more countless husbands will be grateful to you for this service to mankind."

Thanks a thousand times, Mrs. C. D. It's really a pleasure to be of service to you and to the many other ladies who write in. For almost 40 years, I have been trying to play a symphony with pots and pans, because I like to cook and I love good things to eat. Tell me, what other joys are there in this life that are greater than a fine dinner, leisurely eaten?

EAST INDIAN AN ARTIST WITH CURRY.

Years ago I knew an East Indian—his name was Prince Rajah Smile. He had a real smile all right, but I am not sure that he was a real Prince. He worked in the dining room of Rector's, pushing his tray wagon around from table to table offering his curries. They were good, too. Wearing his native costume and preparing the Indian specialties right before the guests was something New York had never seen before. The Prince was so anxious to give local color to his act that he asked if he might bring his little pet cobra along with him, but that part of his act was tabooed.

The Prince did several curries—chicken and shellfish and lamb. He was an artist and proved it because he established quite a following. I think the best curry he did was with chicken. The same curry sauce was served with the lamb or shellfish, the latter meaning lobster, shrimp and crabmeat combined. The preliminary work was done in the kitchen and for his chicken curry he would start as follows:

Singe, wash and dry a three- or four-pound young fowl. Cover with boiling water, to which has been added several outer stalks of celery, one carrot, an onion, a few whole black peppers, a bay leaf or two, a small bunch of parsley and one tablespoon of salt. Bring the water quickly to the boiling point and reduce heat and simmer for say two and one-half hours, until fowl is very tender. Remove meat from bones and cut in edible size pieces. Return bones and skin to broth and continue cooking for another hour. Strain the broth, remove the fat and cool.

Suppose you figure on having three cups of broth. All right. Now melt four tablespoons of butter in a saucepan, and in this butter cook colorless one tablespoon of very finely chopped onions, then add four tablespoons of curry powder and four tablespoons of flour which have been mixed together. Cook slowly, stirring well until thoroughly blended. Add the chicken broth slowly, and do some more stirring. Watch your sauce, so as not to have it too thick nor too thin. When the sauce comes to boiling point add the piece of chicken meat to heat. Now, just before serving, add one cup of cream and stir again.

If you want further to enrich the sauce as well as thicken it, add three egg yolks well beaten, but add them slowly over very low heat, and stir.

CHUTNEY TO GO WITH CURRY.

Now for the trimmings that go with a curry, serve East Indian chutney: One cupful of rolled peanuts, the same amount of grated coconut, and one-half cup of finely chopped green peppers. No curry is complete without boiled rice. Arrange a border of rice on a soup plate. Dish out the curry and then pass the trimmings at the table.

If you fancy a shellfish curry, make the sauce the same way, by using a light-colored stock, chicken or veal stock, and again, if you have left over lamb, the procedure is the same. Sliced hard cooked eggs are often served with a curry sauce. Curry powder can be obtained in most of the grocery stores and is packed in small bottles or tins. If you don't know what curry is, I'll tell you. It consists of upward of 20 different powdered herbs and spices, all grown in India.

The next time you, serve asparagus, cauliflower or broccoli, do it a la Polonaise. Place about one dozen cooked and very hot asparagus on a hot platter. Brown in two tablespoons of butter, one-half cup of bread crumbs. Pour the crumbs over the tips of the asparagus and then sprinkle over the crumbs one hard-cooked egg which has been put through a ricer; and lastly, sprinkle over all one tablespoon of finely chopped parsley.

June 3, 1938

Every now and then noodles with ham appeared on the luncheon menu of Rector's. Here are the ingredients:

One-half pound noodles, 1 slice of raw ham (1 pound), 3 tablespoons olive oil, 1½ cups of stock, 2 onions, 1 carrot, 1 button garlic, ½ cup tomato sauce, salt and pepper.

HOW TO PREPARE NOODLES AND HAM A LA RECTOR.

Cut the ham in thin strips. Put onions, carrot, and garlic through the food chopper or chop finely. Heat olive oil in saucepan and add to it the chopped vegetables and seasonings. Do not let the vegetables brown. Now add the stock, which has been heated with the tomato sauce and let this mixture heat for 15 minutes. Cook the noodles in boiling water for about 10 minutes, drain and arrange them in a circle on a platter, making a nest in the center for the sauce. Mix the noodles well with the sauce right at the table and serve with grated cheese, either Swiss or Parmesan.

Tuna fish cooked in with spaghetti is another combination that is worth trying sometime.

Cook ½ pound spaghetti. Heat ¼ cup of olive oil and to it add 1 teaspoon of finely chopped garlic and 2 tablespoons of finely chopped parsley and cook for several minutes. Now add 1 cupful of tomato sauce, ¼ cup of stock.

Season with salt and pepper. After the spaghetti has been drained add it to the sauce, and also the contents of 1 small can of tuna fish which has been flaked. Mix well and heat thoroughly for about 10 minutes, and serve, as usual, with grated cheese.

MIGHTY GOOD AND INEXPENSIVE.

For an inexpensive dish, serve a veal loaf. It's mighty good eating, I can assure you. Purchase 4 pounds of shank of veal and have the butcher crack the bones in several places. Wipe the meat with a damp cloth and place it in a deep sauce pan with 1 cup of diced carrots, 2 sliced onions and ½ cup of diced celery. Season with 1 teaspoon of salt and ½ teaspoon of pepper. Add 1 quart of boiling water and simmer gently until meat is tender. Drain but reserve the broth. Remove meat from the bones and return undesirable particles and bones to the broth. Simmer the broth until it is reduced to one-half. Skim the top of any fat and strain.

When the veal is cold slice it in edible size pieces and add to the strained broth. Now moisten a round mold with a little oil and decorate the bottom with hard cooked sliced eggs, a few pieces of pimiento, cut in small diamonds, and a few slices of cooked carrots. The artistry of decoration, I shall leave entirely to you. Put the veal mixture into the mold and let it become cold and firm in the refrigerator.

Here's one dish that does not call for gelatin, and remember that the salad dressing which I have just given you won't be a bit hard to take with this veal loaf.

LEMON MOUSSE POPULAR DESSERT.

Here is a dessert that is liked by men as well as the ladies. I have demonstrated it at many of my cooking schools, so perhaps you will enjoy knowing about it, too.

Two tablespoons cornstarch, 1 cup milk, 1 cup sugar, ½ cup lemon juice, 3 egg yolks, and 1 pint cream whipped.

Mix cornstarch with one-quarter cup of sugar. Add milk and cook in top part of double boiler for 15 minutes. Add egg yolks and remaining sugar and cook one minute. Add lemon juice and set aside till cold. Then fold in whipped cream and freeze in chilling unit of mechanical refrigerator for three hours. If you haven't a unit, then put mousse in tightly covered mold and freeze in ice and salt pack, using two parts of finely chopped ice to one part salt. Freeze three hours.

NICE WAY TO SERVE POTATOES.

Potatoes Anna is worth trying sometime. Wash and pare six medium-sized potatoes, trimming them into cylinder shape. Cut them in slices one eighth of an inch thick. You now have rounds of potato slices which should be about one and one-half inches in diameter and one-eighth inch thick. Wash in cold water and dry on a towel. Butter the bottom of a shallow skillet or omelet pan and arrange the potatoes to have the slices overlap each other. The bottom layer becomes the top when the potatoes are turned out, so arrange them nicely, covering the entire bottom of the pan. Spread the layer with softened butter, season each layer with a little salt and pepper and continue to build layers of potatoes and softened butter until about two inches high. Cover pan and cook in moderate oven for one hour. Remove from oven, uncover pan and place a large plate on top, invert pan carefully and there you have a rounded patch of potatoes with a golden browned top.

June 10, 1938

It wasn't so many years ago that sweetbreads were an unknown food. They could be had at the various slaughter houses almost for the asking, but today sweetbreads are considered a delicacy and are prepared in various delicious ways. In making my rounds of the restaurants I notice they are featured on menus much more than ever.

In case you do not know what a sweetbread is, I will tell you briefly. It is the thymus gland of the calf. They come in pairs and when you wish to order them, ask for the veal sweetbreads. Beef breads are also obtainable, but for tenderness they are not to be compared with the veal sweetbreads. Absolute freshness is very important. It is an easily perishable food and preparation for cooking should start at once.

Wash and soak the sweetbreads in cold water. That is the first procedure, then put them in a sauce pan and cover with cold water. Drop in a teaspoon of salt and let boil or parboil for about 10 minutes. Remove the sweetbreads from the boiling water and then drop them into cold water for about 15 minutes.

Sweetbreads, as I explained, come in pairs. Now, after they have been taken out of the cold water, sever the breads and also trim and remove the membranes. Right now, while they are cold, place a weight over them so that they will become flat rather than rounded.

SWEETEREADS BRAISED OR BROILED.

About the nicest way to prepare sweetbreads is to braise them. Parboil, let's say four pair, which means eight pieces (after they have been severed), lard each with three or four thin strips of larding pork. Place the breads in a shallow buttered baking pan and then into a moderate oven. During the cooking, baste occasionally. To keep them moist, add more butter and don't forget to season with a little salt and pepper. Place on a hot platter small rounds of freshly made toast and place on each piece of toast one of the breads.

Now right here I'll tell you of a secret that famous chefs have. They dip a small brush in partly melted glace de viand, which is extract of beef, and brush over the top of each sweetbread a small quantity of this extract. This is for two purposes, first to give a glazed effect on the surface and to add flavor to the sweetbreads. To complete this culinary delight, be sure to serve green peas; it's just an old custom, that's all.

Broiled sweetbreads are good, too. All you have to do is to cut them in half lengthwise, dip them in melted butter, season and then into the boiler. Please remember that the breads should be parboiled, no matter how you decide to cook them. Cold sweetbreads, or in case you have some left over for the next day, can be used in a salad or as a reheat they could be prepared a la Newburg or a la king.

I once visited that delightful little town of Smithfield, situated on the Pagan River in Virginia to find out as much as I could about the razorback hog—what they ate, what they were fed and the process of smoking and curing. One of the foods they eat that gives the Virginia hams such a delicious flavor is peanuts. The hams are smoked by using green hickory and maple wood; a rotted apple tree is usually tossed in as a finishing touch. Curing and aging follow and after one year of aging, hams are ready for shipment.

HOW TO COOK THE HAM OF HAMS.

Now comes the cooking of the ham of hams.

Cover the Virginia ham with cold water and allow to soak overnight. Put the ham in a large pot with boiling water to cover the ham and allow to simmer gently, allowing fifteen minutes to the pound. These hams may weigh anywhere from ten to eighteen pounds. Add to the water in which the ham is cooking one onion, a small bunch of parsley, several outer stalks of celery and leaves, one dozen black peppers, six cloves and several bay leaves.

Leave the ham in the water in which it was cooked until it is sufficiently cooled to handle, then place on a board and peel off the outer skin, using care not to tear the fat. And, between you and me, what a delicious morsel that is! Cover fat with a goodly quantity of brown sugar, mixed with freshly grated bread crumbs. Now stud the surface liberally with whole cloves. Place the ham in a large baking pan and pour around it one quart of apple cider. Now if you don't happen to have any cider around, you have my permission to pour a pint of sherry in the pan. Grape juice also goes well, if you desire it. Baste frequently in a hot oven to give it that appetizing brown glaze.

June 17, 1938

Small fish, weighing from slightly under a pound up to two pounds can be cooked in a certain way that I am sure you will say is the tops. The method as known in France is called en papiotte or in our language paper bag cookery.

The whole idea of cooking fish in paper is that when the fish is cooked you will find that all the flavor has been retained and that in cooking no fish odors can escape—and also you have no pans to wash. Now, here's the way to do it:

The fish—let's say brook trout, perch, lake bass, mackerel or sea bass—are cleaned, but heads and tails are not cut off the fish. Season inside of fish with a little salt and pepper. You will now cut heavy brown unglazed paper oval shape large enough to envelope the fish. Rub paper on both sides with cooking oil. Fold the paper in the center and lay one fish thereon, bring edges together and fold and crimp them until there is no opening in the paper. Repeat this procedure for each fish.

PAPER COOKERY POSSIBLE WITH LARGER FISH. Place the fish on the rack in a moderate oven and bake for 20 to 30 minutes, all depending on the size of the fish. A pound size will cook in about 20 minutes. It would be well to open the oven door several times just to see how things are getting on. No doubt you will observe the paper has become scorched, but have no fear that it will catch fire—the cooking oil on the paper prevents that.

In serving the fish place the envelope intact on the plate and let the diner open it. Now watch what happens. The skin of the fish clings to the paper and there you have as fine a tasting fish you ever put into your mouth.

This so-called paper bag cookery need not be confined exclusively to small fish. I have cut slices of halibut, codfish, salmon, and swordfish and cooked them in this manner with the same fine results. Just try shad roe some time cooked this way and I am sure you will like it better than broiled or sautéed.

A nice sauce to serve with it is Sauce Figaro. To one cup of Hollandaise gradually add one-fourth cup of tomato sauce and one tablespoon of finely chopped parsley and mix well.

CALF'S HEAD POPULAR—RECTOR SPECIALTY.

I do not know how many of my readers would care for calf's head prepared as we did it in Rector's. All I can say is it's worth trying, and you won't be disappointed, either, because it was one of our popular specialties.

Have the butcher cut brain, tongue, and meat from a calf's head. The scalp of the head is considered meat. Place all in a large kettle with cold water to cover and let stand for one hour. Drain off water and remove the meat, tongue, and brains. Now refill the kettle with water and let the water come to a boil. Add to this boiling water one onion studded with several cloves, one dozen black peppercorns, several outer leaves of celery, a small bunch of parsley, one carrot, sliced, and one teaspoon of salt. Put in the kettle the meat only and simmer for one-half hour. Then add the tongue and continue simmering for another hour, then add the brains and again let all simmer together—this time for only 20 minutes.

Remove the brains and let them become cool. Remove skin and membranes from the brains and cut in small pieces, to be used in a sauce which I will tell you about in a moment. Now remove the meat and tongue from the hot water in which they were cooked and arrange neatly on a hot platter. The skin and throat cords should be removed from the tongue.

Vinaigrette dressing is invariably served with calf's head. To make it just add to one cup of French dressing two tablespoons of finely chopped vinegar pickles, one tablespoon of finely chopped chives and if you have not chives use a teaspoon of finely chopped onions and one tablespoon of chopped parsley. Pour the dressing in a small bowl and in it add the brains. Mash and stir until thoroughly mixed. Right now drop in one tablespoon of capers.

Adding the calf's brains to the dressing was a new one on me, until I saw it done right at the table by the maître d'hotel of that very fine hotel in Cannes, France, the Hotel Majestic.

GOOD WAY TO PREPARE CALF'S BRAINS.

All of this which I had to say about calf's head leads up to an inquiry that I received from a lady who said she was very fond of calf's brains and wanted to know a good way to prepare them. I think the nicest way to do them is Sauté Beurre Noir—meaning black butter.

Remove skin and membranes from the brains and then soak them in salted cold water for one-half hour. Drop the brains in boiling water and let simmer for 10 minutes. Remove from the water and let them cool. Put a tablespoon of butter in a saucepan and when the butter becomes hot, place the brains in the pan—that is, one pair of brains—season with salt and pepper and cook for only a few minutes. Remove them carefully onto a hot platter and sprinkle over the brains one tablespoon of finely chopped chives. Add to the remaining butter in the pan one more tablespoon of butter and let it become very hot over a high fire until the butter turns brown and popping. Then add quickly one tablespoon of vinegar and immediately remove pan from heat.

There will be quite a sizzle and a puff of smoke arise when the vinegar and hot butter meet, so do not get too close to the stove, otherwise this very hot, combination might sputter and burn your hand.

Pour this sizzling hot sauce right over the brains and, voila! you have a food that will be received by a couple of yum-yums and very likely an oh, la, la! Here I go out the door to the butcher's for calf's brains. I will cook them Au Beurre Noir. That's my dinner tonight.

June 24, 1938

A few years ago, I had charge of the cuisine of sixty-odd dining cars of an important transcontinental railroad. The kitchens of these dining cars are so small that it is amazing how so much food can be prepared, with so few cooks.

A standard diner carries four cooks—the chef, second, third, and fourth cooks. The average seating capacity is 36, although I am told on some of the super trains, as many as 48 can be served. It is not unusual to serve 100 or more passengers during the meal hours. These dining car kitchens are fully equipped in every way, every inch of space is utilized, and there's a place for everything.

I have never been able to figure out how these four men in the kitchen, although carefully trained, can turn out so many meals, with so little confusion. They move fast all right, but they can't move far, the space is so small. One evening I went into the kitchen to speak to the chef, and to show you how crowded they all are, just started to talk with him, he dropped his pencil, and as I stooped to pick it up, he pushed me right out of the kitchen. Maybe that was his way of letting me know I wasn't wanted in there.

Working in large kitchens such as they have in the Waldorf-Astoria or the Stevens Hotel in Chicago, serving banquets of 3,000 or more, is no greater task than the four boys in the kitchen of a diner have doing three services daily on this long run. The railroads in this country lose hundreds of thousands of dollars annually in the dining car department, but they no doubt figure that good food and service is a big asset for passenger travel. And that reminds me of the concessionaire at the country fair in England who explained: "What I lose in the swinging boats I make up in the merry-go-round."

HOT BRAN BREAD GOOD ANY MEAL.

One of my chefs was a chap named Martin. He turned out the best hot bran bread I ever tasted. You can serve it for breakfast, luncheon or dinner, and I can assure you it will go over big with all members of the family. Here's the recipe:

Thin Bran Bread.

Three-quarters cup butter, ¾ cup sugar, 3 eggs, 3 cups bran, 1 ½ cups milk, 1 cup flour, ½ cup yellow corn meal, 2 teaspoons baking powder, ½ teaspoon salt, 1 cup seedless raisins (optional).

Cream butter and sugar together and whip until light and fluffy. Add eggs one at a time, beating well after each addition. Add bran; let stand while you sift together the flour, corn meal, baking powder and salt. Then add the sifted dry ingredients to first mixture, alternately with milk. If raisins are used in the recipe, prepare them by covering with boiling hot water and let them simmer for 10 minutes; drain and add them to the recipe along with the bran. Spread mixture in large shallow greased pan to one-third inch thickness. Bake in moderate oven (375 degrees) for 20 minutes.

This recipe, as you will observe, is worked out on the cake mixing method, and because of that, this thin hot bran bread when baked becomes light and ever so tender.

REAL SHORTCAKE IS MADE WITH BISCUIT DOUGH.

Old-fashioned strawberry shortcake is an American institution, and if it is not made with the genuine biscuit shortcake, it's—well, something else. Call it what you may, I never saw such luscious, juicy, fine tasting berries as are in the markets today; and right now, let me say that this crack French pastry chef in Rector's used the following recipe with overwhelming success. Here we go:

Wash thoroughly 2 quarts of strawberries in cold water. Hull the berries carefully and drop them in a large bowl. Sprinkle over them one and one-half cups of granulated sugar and crush them lightly. Now don't mash, please. Mix them well so that they may all be coated with a little of the sugar. Place the berries in a cool place for about one hour. Now let's make the shortcake:

Two cups flour, 2 teaspoons baking powder, 2 tablespoons sugar, ½ teaspoon salt, ¼ cup butter, 1 egg well beaten, ½ cup milk.

Mix and sift together dry ingredients; cut in butter. Add well beaten egg and milk, and with a knife or spatula cut until you have a soft dough. Toss onto lightly floured board, pat and roll very thin (about inch thick). Spread half the dough with melted butter and fold the other half on it. If one large shortcake is desired, cut the dough to fit into a pan that size. For individual shortcakes, follow recipe as explained and cut in rounds or 3-inch squares. Bake in hot oven (450 degrees) 12 to 15 minutes. Split, spread with soft butter. Cover bottom part of shortcake with crushed berries, put top of shortcake in place and pour remaining berries over all. Serve with heavy cream, or whipped if you prefer.

MERINGUE IN PLACE OF CREAM.

Now, if you would like a variation in your strawberry shortcake, try a strawberry meringue over the cake and berries, instead of the traditional cream. Follow instructions for shortcake and berries as already explained, then heap strawberry meringue over cake and berries. Nice for a change. Here is the recipe for strawberry meringue:

Put into a well-chilled bowl 1 cup of crushed strawberries, ¾ cup of powdered sugar and 2 egg whites. Place bowl in a larger one containing ice water and beat mixture with a rotary beater until it is stiff enough to cut with a knife. Then whip in 4 tablespoons of extra heavy cream. Cover shortcake and serve. In beating a mixture like this, it is well to cover bowl with oiled paper to prevent spattering outside.

July 1, 1938

In the kitchens of large hotels and restaurants they usually have an abundance of stock. I mean beef stock or chicken stock. A greater part of the stock is reduced and after it is clarified it becomes bouillon or consommé. It is kept in the refrigerators and because of the concentration in cooking, it quickly jells when it becomes cold.

The jellied bouillon has many uses, especially during the summer months. Jellied soups are very popular. All aspic dishes call for this jellied bouillon. The dark-colored bouillon is made from beef and the light-colored bouillon is made from chicken or veal.

To give you a better idea of what is meant by an aspic, I will explain a simple one. It is done first by poaching eggs. Set the eggs aside to cool. Now line individual shallow earthenware or glass casseroles with slices of cooked ham, cut round and about three inches in diameter. Place carefully one egg on each slice of ham. Decorate the egg, in a fancy way, with pimientos or green peppers cut in small diamond shape. Melt the bouillon, just enough so it will pour and then pour this bouillon over the eggs and place in refrigerator to chill.

There are that can be prepared under heading of aspics, such as slices of chicken, slices of smoked tongue and other cold cuts. Of course, I do not expect housewives to have in their kitchens gallons and gallons of stock, and that is why gelatin is used to make these jellies, soups and aspics at home.

DELICIOUS DISH FOR HOT DAY

Jellied chicken salad is a delightful dish to anticipate on a hot day. It is especially tempting when made from the breast of fowl only, but also a treat when made with a combination of the white and dark meat. The first procedure is to select a plump fowl weighing about five pounds. Have it drawn at the market; also have the head and feet chopped off. The fowl is not to be disjointed, as for this particular recipe it is better to have it left whole. Remember that when you want cold chicken meat for salads or sandwiches always cook the fowl whole, as the meat will slice to much better advantage.

A soup pot or sauce pan with depth rather than width is the ideal receptacle to cook the fowl in. Cover fowl with about two quarts of water, add the usual soup bunch, consisting of celery, parsley, leek or onion and a carrot or two. Bring to a quick boil, then reduce heat and let simmer for about two and one-half hours until the fowl is tender. The last half hour of cooking add one teaspoon of salt. Let fowl stand in broth until cool. Remove to cutting board and cut off enough meat to give three cupfuls. Cut the meat in edible-sized pieces and let marinate in one-third of a cup of French dressing for 15 or 20 minutes. In the meanwhile prepare the balance of the recipe:

Two tablespoons gelatin, ¼ cup cold water, 1 quart chicken stock, ½ cup celery, thinly sliced, 1 teaspoon capers (optional).

Soak gelatin in cold water for 10 minutes. Skim fat off chicken stock, bring to boiling point and pour it on soaked gelatin, stirring until dissolved. Strain through a double thickness of cheese cloth and let stand in a pan of ice until it partially congeals. Then add the marinated chicken, celery, and capers—a little at a time—so that it is thoroughly mixed through the jelly. Turn mixture into large or individual molds which have been lightly oiled. Chill in refrigerator until set. Unmold carefully onto crisp lettuce leaves. Garnish with quartered hard-cooked egg and quartered tomatoes with skins removed. Served with mayonnaise.

MOLDED SALMON SALAD SUMMER FAVORITE.
Another hot weather favorite is Molded Salmon Salad. Here is how: One tablespoon gelatin, 2 tablespoons cold water, 1 ½ cups fish stock or water, 2 tablespoons lemon juice, light pinch of cayenne pepper, 1 tablespoon salt, salmon (one pound can), 1 cup celery (finely chopped), 2 tablespoons green peppers (finely chopped), 2 tablespoons pimiento (finely chopped), and ¾ cup mayonnaise.

Soak gelatin in cold water for 10 minutes. Pour boiling hot fish stock or water on soaked gelatin, stirring until dissolved. Strain through a double thickness of cheese cloth. Add strained lemon juice, cayenne and salt, and let stand in a pan of ice until it starts to congeal. While this is taking place remove bones and skin from salmon and break into flakes. Combine flaked salmon, celery, green peppers, pimientos, and mayonnaise and add this mixture to the congealed gelatin and mix gently. Turn into lightly oiled mold and place in refrigerator to chill. Serve on a bed of crisp lettuce, garnished with sliced pickled beets and small vinegar pickles cut fan shape. This is done by thinly slicing the pickles from the tip to one-quarter of an inch of the stem end, then spread fan shape.

FRUIT SALAD PART FROZEN.
Now here is a fruit salad recipe for those who have a mechanical refrigerator:

One orange, 1 banana, 1 cup white grapes, 2 slices pineapple, ½ cup maraschino cherries, ½ cup mayonnaise, ½ pint cream.

Cut orange in half and with a small sharp knife remove sections, also seeds. Peel and thinly slice banana. Cut grapes in halves and remove seeds. Shred the pineapple and cut maraschino cherries in halves. Whip the cream and fold it into the mayonnaise. Then add the prepared fruit and turn into freezing tray until partially frozen. Cut in squares and serve on bed of crisp lettuce.

NICE WITH COLD CUTS.

Now the next recipe is not a meal in itself but it is a dandy supplement to a platter of cold cuts—tomato aspic salad: Soak two tablespoons of gelatin in one-half cup of water for ten minutes. In the meanwhile cook together one quart of canned tomatoes, two tablespoons of finely chopped onion, one-half cup of celery leaves, one bay leaf, one teaspoon of salt and a light pinch of cayenne pepper. Let this simmer together for 15 minutes. Remove from fire, add two tablespoons of vinegar, one teaspoon of powdered sugar and soaked gelatin, stirring until dissolved. Strain into lightly oiled molds (preferably tomato shape) and when thoroughly chilled serve on a bed of lettuce with mayonnaise.

July 8, 1938

Judging from the number of requests I have received for a recipe for French pancakes, better known as Crepes Suzette, it would be best to let all my readers have it.

The last time I prepared this dish was out in Hollywood, and it was done on a set in one of the large movie studios. An exact replica of the old Rector's was built for something like $60,000. Lot of money for props, and after they got through shooting scenes for only five days, they busted up Rector's in a few hours. The movie people gave a big party as a final gesture to the passing of Rector's. I was asked to prepare for the honored guests Crepes Suzette, and there I found myself back in the restaurant business again, but not for long.

FRENCH PANCAKES SERVED AS A DESSERT.
A lot of people think that French pancakes are something like our own flapjacks. Well, they are, except they are ever so much thinner and are served strictly as a dessert. I know of no food that attracted more attention when served in the dining room of Rector's. There's plenty of showmanship in doing this dish right at your own dining table.

If you desire to go in for Crepes Suzette in a big way I would suggest you purchase the proper equipment. It resembles a chafing dish, with an alcohol burner and a large flat pan, which sets directly over the burner. Any one of the large hotel and restaurant equipment houses handles them. If you have a chafing dish with direct heat, it will answer the purpose all right, but I would rather work with the gadget that is made for doing Crepes Suzette only. The first thing we do is to make the pancake batter.

One cup flour, 2 tablespoons sugar, ½ teaspoon salt, 1 cup milk, 3 eggs, unbeaten, butter for frying.

Mix flour, sugar and salt, eggs and milk slowly, stirring until very smooth. Then strain the mixture. French pancakes are made one at a time. Butter a small frying pan, about five inches in diameter. If you have two or three of these small pans so much the better. You can turn them out faster. Pour a small amount of batter in the buttered pan, just enough to cover bottom of pan. You see, the secret of cooking these pancakes is to have them very thin. Hence the name "crepes." It would be well to experiment in cooking a sample batch. Cut the recipe in thirds; this will make seven pancakes, using a tablespoon of batter for each pancake. In putting the batter in the little frying pan tilt it so the batter will spread out evenly to edge of pan. These little pancakes brown quickly and they should be turned with a spatula. Keep on cooking them until batter has been used, greasing the frying pan each time with soft paper and very little butter.

MORE SHOWMANSHIP WITH SUZETTE.

Now comes the Suzette part of this wonderful dessert creation. About two hours before you start cooking the pancakes prepare a butter as follows: Cream into ½ pound of butter the grated rind of 1 orange and 1 lemon, 2 tablespoons of granulated sugar and the juice of ½ orange. After you have prepared the "butter" place it in the refrigerator, until needed. Set the Crepes Suzette chafing dish before you at the dining table. Also have alongside of you the stack of thin pancakes (which you have made in the kitchen), the orange butter and three liqueurs, not liquors. A bottle of benedictine, a bottle of grand marnier and a bottle of cognac. No, my dear readers, we are not going to use the whole three bottles, just a little of each.

Now watch! Ignite the alcohol burner and place the pan over it. Drop on the pan two tablespoons of the prepared orange butter. When the butter has melted add four pancakes, and with a spoon and fork push and turn the pancakes around to heat thoroughly. Right now, pour quickly over the pancakes two tablespoons of each of the liqueurs. Ignite the liqueurs with a lighted match and now a beautiful colored flame will arise. More showmanship! Now fold the pancakes and fold again so that they will be sort of triangular in shape. Keep spooning the sauce over them. Serve three or four to a portion, with the sauce, and then proceed with the next batch of pancakes and repeat the operation.

We didn't always use the liqueurs in Rector's for the sauce. Perhaps you would fancy a chocolate sauce which could be served after the pancakes are heated in the prepared orange butter. We also did them another way, by spreading each pancake with jelly and then rolling them instead of folding them. Powdered sugar was then sprinkled over the top.

BAKED RICE AND PINEAPPLE PUDDING.

Rice and fruit combinations are most popular for family desserts, so I thought you would like to try baked rice and pineapple pudding. Cook one cup of rice in two quarts of rapidly boiling salted water until tender—about 15 minutes. Drain; pour fresh hot water over rice and again drain. Butter a medium-sized pudding dish. Spread a layer of rice on the bottom, sprinkle lightly with brown sugar and dot with small pieces of butter, then a layer of chopped or shredded pineapple. Continue these layers until rice and pineapple has been used. Rice layers should be about one-half inch high. Pour pineapple syrup over the top and bake in moderate oven (uncovered) for 20 minutes.

Chill and serve with plain sweet cream or if you would like a cream sauce here is a very nice one: Separate two eggs; beat yolks with one-eighth teaspoon of salt. Beat whites with one-third cup of powdered sugar until foamy. Pour one-half pint of heavy cream over egg yolks and beat with rotary beater until thick, adding one-half teaspoon of vanilla. Combine by folding beaten egg whites into cream mixture.

July 15, 1938

Europeans consider cheese a very important food, all the way from the peasants up to those born to the purple. The famous wine testers from England eat cheese on a small piece of bread and chase it down with mouthful of wine in order to get the full flavor of the wine.

I once knew a Frenchman named Henri Fournier. You may recall him as one of the pioneer automobile race drivers. We had lunch together one day in Paris and because he wasn't feeling so well, he ordered just three things—a whole Camembert cheese, a couple of French rolls and a bottle of good red Bordeaux wine. Right there and then I was introduced to this delightful combination.

Who doesn't like cheese? Take, for example, those fine cooks in France, England, Germany, and other countries; and chefs, by the way, are good judges of food. Well, they never fail to have cheese at the completion of lunch and dinner. I know, because I have eaten with them hundreds of times. Several kinds of cheese are served, not merely one kind.

STILTON CHEESE TREATED À LA RECTOR.
Way back in the gay nineties, that fine gentleman, the late George Horace Lorimer was then Secretary to P. D. Armour of Chicago. Years later, while I was visiting Mr.

Lorimer in his offices of the *Saturday Evening Post,* we got to talking about food. He reminded me that the Stilton cheese that he got in my father's restaurant in Chicago was the most delicious cheese he ever tasted. He knew, of course, that it was treated in a way to bring out the real flavor. So when I returned home I went to one of the big wholesale cheese houses and selected a real fine Stilton cheese, not too ripe, to treat it a la Rector and present it to Mr. Lorimer.

These English Stilton cheeses come in earthen crocks with an earthen lid. The first thing I did was to bore a hole down the center with a cheese tester and when the cheese tester is withdrawn, it leaves a hole about one-half inch right down to the bottom of the crock. Then I filled the opening with a small glassful of sherry and replaced the lid. The next day I gave it another "drink" but this time it was port wine. I repeated the operation daily for 10 days, alternating with sherry and port. The wine naturally will seep through the cheese. Keep the cheese in a cool place at all times.

A few days before I sent this cheese to Mr. Lorimer, I wrote him a note informing him that it would soon be on its way. He replied immediately expressing his delight and terminated his note with this cryptic remark, "I trust, my dear Rector, there is no esoteric meaning attaching this gift."

Another delightful cheese combination that epicureans enjoyed in Rector's was fresh Bartlett pears cut in sections, with a dab of soft Camembert cheese. Soft Camembert cheese was known as "running south."

Cheese is a food that you should always have on hand. For a quick snack, especially when unexpected guests arrive, I know of no food that is more acceptable. A good-sized chunk of our own American cheese wrapped in a damp cloth and kept in the refrigerator, is a real food asset. It can be served or prepared in many ways.

RECIPE FOR THE POPULAR WELSH RABBIT.

All au gratin dishes call for grated cheese. Welsh rabbits and cheese souffles are very popular. In making a Welsh rabbit a medium sharp American cheese is what you will need and here is the recipe:

Slice one pound of American store cheese in thin pieces of finely shredded. Melt two tablespoons of butter in a saucepan, then put in the cheese. Stir and just as soon as the cheese starts to melt pour in one-half cup of ale or beer along with the seasonings. The seasonings are: One teaspoon of salt, one teaspoon of dry mustard and one teaspoon of paprika. Remember to whip or stir constantly until the cheese is bubbling hot. Have ready at hand some piping hot Welsh rabbit dishes with a piece of freshly made hot toast in each dish. Put a small piece of butter under each slice of toast, as this will prevent the toast from sticking to the hot dish. Now if you would fancy what is known as a "short" rabbit then add two slightly beaten eggs when rabbit mixture is bubbling hot. Stir rapidly and serve at once.

GOLDEN BUCK CALLS FOR DIFFERENT SEASONINGS.

Golden Buck is popular, too. It is made with different seasonings than the Welsh rabbit recipe and is served with a poached egg on top:

Two tablespoons butter, 1 pound American cheese (shredded), 2 teaspoons Worcestershire sauce, few grains cayenne pepper, ⅓ cup ale or beer, 2 eggs (optional), 1 teaspoon salt.

Melt butter, add cheese and stir until partially melted. Add seasonings and beer gradually, stirring constantly until smooth and bubbling hot. Serve on toast and drop a poached egg on top of each portion. A Scotch Woodcock is the Welsh rabbit recipe but the toast is spread with anchovy paste or covered with anchovy fillets. The hot rabbit is then poured over the anchovy toast and served with two anchovy fillets placed crosswise on top. A good quality cheese is most important for a rabbit. Also important is to serve it piping hot on very hot dishes.

CHEESE SOUFFLE ALWAYS WELCOME DISH.
Another old-lime favorite cheese dish that is usually received at the luncheon or dinner table with glee is cheese souffle:

Three tablespoons butter, 3 tablespoons flour, 1 teaspoon salt, ½ teaspoon dry mustard, 1 cup milk (scalded), 1 cup grated cheese, 3 egg yolks, 3 egg whites.

Melt butter, add flour, salt, and mustard and stir until blended. Add hot milk gradually, stirring constantly until smooth. Then add the grated cheese. Remove from fire and stir in well beaten egg yolks. Let mixture cool and fold in stiffly beaten egg whites. Pour into a buttered baking dish. Place the dish in a pan of hot water and bake in a moderate oven about 35 minutes. Souffle should be served immediately.

July 22, 1938

It's a good idea during the summer months to prepare foods that are not going to require too much time spent in the kitchen. I have in mind, particularly a smoked beef tongue. Yesterday afternoon, I purchased a small tongue, which weighed exactly three and one-half pounds. Of course, they come heavier and the size that you desire depends upon the number in your family.

Boiled beef tongue, along with the proverbial spinach, served hot, is a hearty and satisfying meal in itself. The whole tongue need not be consumed at this one meal alone. The idea is to make two meals out of it. Cold sliced tongue with a goodly bowl of salad, is worth while sitting down to. Other cold cuts can be added, such as ham, corned beef, and cheese.

On several occasions I have purchased in food stores sliced cold tongue and each time I have been disappointed. Invariably it's tough and it is usually cut too thin. A beef tongue should be very tender and the trick is in the cooking. Here's a food that must be boiled very, very slowly. Simmering is the better word for it.

Tongues like hams are lightly cured or smoked nowadays and do not require previous soaking in cold water. They can be started to cook at once in cold water to cover and when simmering point is reached one can forget for several hours that a part of a swell dinner is well on the way. In other words it is a food that almost cooks itself, as it requires no attention whatsoever from the housewife. It is a good recipe to remember if you have occasion to absent yourself from home of an afternoon.

SMOKED BEEF TONGUE, SAUCE PIQUANTE.

When smoked beef tongue appeared on the menu of Rector's it was always coupled with sauce piquante and white bean puree. This is the recipe I want to give you today.

Cover beef tongue with cold water. Add several sprigs of parsley, one medium-sized onion, one bay leaf, a large piece of lemon rind, three whole cloves, and about 10 peppercorns. Bring to boiling point and let boil five minutes. Then lower heat and let simmer (a point where there is the faintest ripple in the water) until cooked—about four hours. Remove tongue to cutting board; when cool enough to handle trim off thick skin and throat cords. Place tongue on large hot platter and pour sauce around tongue.

The foundation for sauce piquante calls for a cup of thick brown sauce. A restaurant kitchen, of course, has this sauce on hand at all times. You may have some on hand too. If so, use it. If you have to make it, then the short cut is to use glaze de viande (beef extract) or a can of bouillon.

Two tablespoons butter, 2 tablespoons flour, 1 tablespoon beef extract, 1 cup boiling water, ½ cup tongue water (strained), 3 tablespoons tarragon vinegar, 2 tablespoons vinegar pickle (finely chopped), 1 teaspoon shallot (finely chopped), 1 teaspoon capers (finely chopped), 1 teaspoon parsley (finely chopped).

Brown the butter, add browned flour and stir until blended. Add beef extract which has been dissolved in boiling hot water and stir until smooth and boiling point is reached. Now in another small saucepan put the tongue water and tarragon vinegar along with the finely chopped shallots or onions and let boil uncovered until reduced to one-half the quantity. Then stir into the thick brown along with the vinegar pickle, capers and parsley, all finely chopped. Sauce may be held for 15 or 20 minutes at warm part of range, but do not allow to boil again. Serve half the sauce around tongue and balance in sauceboat.

TO MAKE THIS DISH COMPLETE

A puree of white beans and fresh spinach will make this dish complete. The bean puree is made from our dry white navy beans. The beans are covered with cold water and soaked for several hours. The water is then drained off and fresh cold water is poured over them. A medium-sized onion is added and they are slowly brought to simmering point. They are to be cooked at this low heat until the skins bursts and the bean feels soft enough to mash easily.

It is rather difficult to give the exact time for cooking a dried vegetable as the age has a lot to do with it. However, after one hour of simmering it would be a good idea to test a few and this will tell you if they need 30 minutes longer or possibly another hour of simmering.

When they are soft to the touch, drain off water and while they are hot, force them through a fine sieve. To every cupful of bean puree add a tablespoon of butter with salt and pepper to taste and whip together over hot fire. This is a particularly nice puree to serve with boiled tongue or ham.

You all know how to cook spinach, but if you would like a different flavor sometime add a few grains of nutmeg to it after it is cooked and finely chopped and seasoned with salt and a piece of fresh butter.

July 29, 1938

The nearest I ever got to the Orient was Seattle, Wash., where I met a Chinese restaurateur named Mar Dong. In the so-called Chinatown of that city, Mar Dong conducts a hotel and restaurant. Until I became acquainted with his superb food, I never had any great desire for Chinese dishes.

Before I give you some of Mr. Dong's famous Chinese recipes, I want to tell you of a little experience I had a few years ago when I happened to be in Baltimore. I was walking up Fayette Street, one of the main thoroughfares, when, lo and behold, I saw a great big electric sign being tested out. It had colored lights with dragons intertwining around this huge sign. The name on the sign was Rector's in large, bold letters.

I thought it would be fun to go and see what it all about. There was plenty of activity going on inside. Carpets were being laid, chairs and tables were being set up; in fact, I soon found out they were getting ready to open the following day.

I wanted more information so I asked, "Who's opening this restaurant?" and was promptly told that the Chinese who was standing near by was the proprietor. I walked over to him and introduced myself. He was most cordial and right there extended to me an invitation to the opening.

What I wanted to find out was what right did he have to call this Chinese restaurant Rectors. He replied in perfect English and in all seriousness informed me he had every right to call it Rector's because, he said, "My middle name in Chinese is Rector." Can you imagine? I let it go at that, getting a good laugh out of it.

Getting back to Mar Dong's restaurant in Seattle, the dinner which he served me was known as a mandarin's dinner.

Bird-nest soup was the first course and upon inquiry I learned that the base or substance of this prized delicacy was found in swallows' nests in Northern China. The nest is soaked for several hours in water to cover and then picked over to remove any bits of straw or feathers. It is then started to cook with fresh water and a bit of ginger root.

After one hour of cooking it is drained and covered with a primary broth which is made from a combination of chicken and lean pork. To one pound of chicken, which has been cut in several pieces, and one pound of lean pork, three pints of water is added and this is allowed to simmer until all essence has been extracted into the broth. The bird's nest and broth are then brought to a boil and allowed to simmer for about 30 minutes. It is then seasoned to taste and a garnish of finely chopped ham and diced cooked chicken is added. The broth is slightly thickened with cornstarch and water and served piping hot.

If you serve it to the family don't tell them what it is until after dinner. They will enjoy it no doubt, but it is just as well to keep it a secret.

Another course that we had resembled our type of omelette, but much more complicated. We must give the Chinese credit for the great variety of foods used to make an egg dish. Here is the recipe:

CHINESE OMELETTE

One small onion, finely chopped; ¼ cup mushrooms, finely chopped, ¼ cup fresh shrimp or crabmeat, finely chopped; ¼ cup cooked chicken, finely chopped; ¼ cup cooked ham, finely chopped, and 6 eggs well beaten.

The onions and mushrooms are cooked together in a tablespoon of vegetable oil for several minutes. Then the shellfish, chicken, and ham are added and stirred for about one minute to mix and heat. Then the well-beaten eggs are poured over the top and cooked as an omelette. This is a tasty dish and all the ingredients are known and adaptable to the American kitchen.

I suppose that you will want a recipe for chop suey since we are discussing Chinese food. This dish is not known in China, but derives its name from the variety of foods which is cut in small pieces and served in a thickened sauce. However, the method of combining a small amount of meat with a large amount of vegetables is Chinese cookery from a long way back, having its origin in the teachings of Confucius.

Chinese cooks are very methodical in their work and whether the cutting of meat and vegetables calls for slicing, dicing, or shredding, you may be sure that the pieces are evenly cut and of uniform size.

Fried foods are used a great deal in Chinese cookery and for this purpose sesame seed or peanut oil is used. These oils impart a flavor peculiar to this type of food. However, for deep fat frying all Chinese cooks will tell you that they use lard.

CHOP SUEY.

One frying chicken (2½ to 3 pounds), 2 cups celery, sliced crosswise, 2 cups onions, coarsely chopped, 1 cup bean sprouts, drained, ½ cup water chestnuts, shredded, ½ cup mushrooms, sliced, 1 cup bamboo shoots, shredded.

Cut the raw chicken breasts, legs and second joints into rather small pieces. Make a chicken stock from the bones, skin, and wings by covering with cold water and a pinch of salt, and simmering for about one hour. With the broth prepared proceed with the recipe. Put the chicken meat into a hot oiled frying pan and cook on all sides until heated but not browned. Then add the vegetables and stir them gently to absorb some of the oil. Use only enough peanut or vegetable oil to keep the chicken and vegetables from sticking to the pan. Let cook together for about five minutes then add strained hot chicken stock to cover. Cover pan tightly and let simmer over low heat for about 30 minutes. Thicken with cornstarch moistened with cold water and cook for a minute or two longer. Remove from heat and stir in one tablespoon of Chinese soy sauce. Serve with plain boiled rice and additional soy sauce at the table.

All the Chinese ingredients I have mentioned in this recipe are procurable in cans or bottles in all Chinese grocery stores and many American stores.

August 5, 1938

The word "peach" signifies about "tops" in more than the luscious fruit alone. The usage of the word to describe a perfect or beautiful thing has crept into our vocabulary until today we apply it to things or people that we like.

Some of our patrons insisted on having peaches in January or February, so we imported the luscious fruit from Africa—which pleased their vanity and satisfied their palate. When a diner asked for something rare or out of season in a loud, expensive voice we lent a sympathetic ear and sent the Rector market basket on its flight.

There were so many foods that were imported in those days that appear in our markets today as quite commonplace. For years Belgium had an uncontested monopoly on endive, and we were absolutely dependent on France for artichokes, mushrooms, and many green vegetables. Avocado pears were shipped from South America and commanded about a dollar apiece.

Quite a different story today with our own Southern states and California growing practically every known fruit and vegetable, keeping our tables well supplied at very little cost the year around.

PEACH CONDE DELICIOUS SUMMER DESSERT. Not forgetting that I had in mind at the beginning to give you several peach recipes, suppose we start off with Peach

Conde. Select large fine peaches of uniform size, allowing one peach for each portion. Remove the skins by dropping the peaches into boiling hot water for one minute. Drain off the water and with a small, sharp knife carefully remove the skins.

Meanwhile prepare a vanilla-flavored syrup in which to poach the peaches. Let's say you will prepare six peaches, therefore you will need this amount of syrup: Two cups of sugar, two cups of water and a small piece of vanilla pod or bean, boiled together for five minutes. The peeled peaches are then dropped into the syrup and gently poached for eight or ten minutes. Let them stay in the syrup until thoroughly chilled.

The rice for this dessert is cooked in a double boiler. Into the top part of a double boiler put one and one-half cups of water. Bring to boiling point over direct heat and gradually add, while stirring with a fork, three-quarters of a cup of washed rice. Let boil five minutes. Put the top part of the boiler into the lower part and steam for about 15 minutes or until the rice has absorbed the water. Then add one pint of milk, one-quarter cup of sugar, a large piece of lemon rind and a tablespoon of butter. Continue steaming until milk is absorbed and rice is soft. Remove from heat and thicken rice with four egg yolks lightly beaten. Stir the yolks gently into the rice, taking care to have them evenly mixed. Let cool.

Now for the raspberry syrup and our Peach Conde will be complete. Purchase a No. 2 size can of raspberries, as this size contains about the amount of juice you will need. Place large strainer over saucepan; empty contents of can into strainer and let juice drain through without mashing fruit. Measure juice and to each cupful add two cups of sugar. Bring to boiling point and let boil for five minutes, stirring occasionally. Remove from fire and skim top of froth. Pour into jar and when cool place in refrigerator until needed. To serve the dessert make a border or bed of the sweet rice (discard lemon rind) and place the drained peaches on top. Coat each peach with one tablespoon of the raspberry syrup.

PEACH MELBA FAVORITE AND EASY TO PREPARE. Another peach favorite was Peach Melba and this will be easy for you to prepare since we have discussed the poaching of peaches in vanilla syrup and the making of raspberry syrup. In serving this dessert it is a good idea to cut a small round of sponge or plain butter cake to fit the bottom of individual dessert dishes. The cake is then evenly covered with a layer of vanilla ice cream and a whole peach, which has been poached in vanilla syrup and drained, placed on top. This raspberry syrup is then poured over the peach.

This dessert isn't always made with the cake base, but I think that you will find it a good idea, as it builds the dessert up and holds it at an attractive stage for some time.

Maraschino liqueur and fresh grated coconut make a grand combination when served on sliced peaches. The ripe peaches are sliced section fashion—that is, cutting them from the outside to the center. A tablespoon of Maraschino liqueur is poured over each portion and fresh grated coconut covers the top. Sweet heavy cream is served with this dessert, but that is passed at the table.

CANNING PEACHES ON A SMALL SCALE. Perhaps you would like to can some peaches for later on. Here is a recipe worked out on a small scale and will only take a few minutes of your time. It will provide you with two full quarts of canned peaches. Take advantage of the peach crop from time to time and stock the pantry shelves with this delicious fruit that we have for so short a time.

Purchase five pounds of fine peaches of uniform size. Scald them with boiling hot water for one minute and drain. Carefully remove skins and cut in halves, discarding the stone. Meanwhile prepare a medium syrup by boiling together for 10 minutes two pounds of sugar and five cups of water. When syrup has boiled 10 minutes drop in peach halves and cook until fruit can be easily pierced with a fork. Have ready the sterilized jars and covers. Adjust rubbers on jars, fill to overflowing with fruit and seal at once.

Don't forget your own favorite peach recipes for shortcake, pie, cobbler, steamed puddings, cakes, and ice cream. Serve these tempting desserts often while the peach season is on.

August 12, 1938

The biggest eater who ever came into Rector's was the famous Diamond Jim Brady. I recall that one of his favorite foods was a double sirloin steak sprinkled with lamb chops. There were other big eaters, too—all over the country—such as champion egg eaters, pie eaters, oyster eaters, and hot-dog eaters, but few of them could compare with the gastronomic feats of Diamond Jim.

When I look back in the past generation it was a mark of distinction to have a topography. A goodly waistline for men and a wasp waistline for women was stylish. Corporation monarchs of today are thin enough to be poor. As a restaurateur, it was my business to sell food; the more food consumed, the bigger the profits. That, I will admit, was a selfish view, but at that the patrons always got a good run for their money, without being gouged. Today people are eating more sensibly, particularly in one respect, and that is moderation.

An easy dinner to prepare and one that requires very little attention is good old reliable chicken fricassee. Serve Southern spoon bread with it for a change or small baking powder biscuits which are quickly cooked in a hot oven. Cornbread is good too with this type of dinner, so if it should strike your fancy to make a batch I'll include my favorite cornbread you. Let's do the fricassee first:

CHICKEN FRICASSEE.

Have a plump fowl disjointed into pieces. Singe, remove any feathers and wash in cold water. Put the chicken in a stewpan, add one clove of garlic, several sprigs of parsley, one small onion, a few celery tops and boiling water to cover. Simmer gently until chicken is tender, which usually takes about two and one-half hours. Season with salt when chicken is half cooked. Lift pieces of chicken onto a hot platter while making the gravy. Strain chicken stock (there should be about three cups) and skim off fat.

In another saucepan melt three tablespoons of butter, blend in four tablespoons of flour and gradually pour in the hot chicken stock, stirring until perfectly smooth and boiling point is reached. At this point we always add two or three beaten egg yolks to obtain a yellow fricassee. Do not allow the gravy to boil after you have added the yolks. Pour hot gravy over the chicken and serve with plain boiled rice and green peas.

SOUTHERN CORNBREAD.

Two cups cornmeal, 1 cup flour, 3 teaspoons baking powder, 2 tablespoons sugar, 1 teaspoon salt, 2 eggs, 1½ cups milk, 3 tablespoons melted butter.

Mix and sift dry ingredients. Beat eggs and gradually add milk and melted butter. Pour liquid mixture into sifted dry mixture and with a knife or spatula cut the batter back and forth. Pour into well-greased shallow baking pan, brush top with melted butter and bake in moderate oven 25 to 30 minutes.

RECTOR'S CHERISHED
RECIPE FOR SUNDAY MORNING.

While we are on the subject of hot breads I thought you might like my cherished recipe for Sunday morning popovers. The reason I have entitled them thus is because, unfortunately, that seems the only morning in the week when time permits the making of this glorious hot bread.

Three eggs, ½ teaspoon salt, 2 cups milk, 1½ cups flour.

Beat eggs well, add salt and milk and beat well together, using an egg beater. Then cut and fold in flour until mixed. Pour batter into sizzling hot well-greased iron popover pans. Bake in hot oven (450 degrees) for 15 minutes. Then reduce heat to 350 degrees and bake for 25 minutes longer. Popovers will more than double when baked, so allow for this when putting the batter in the popover pans; have them half filled, and when they leave the oven they will be baked high above the pans with a hollow center and a crisp outside crust. It is important not to open oven during the baking.

SPOON BREAD.

Now for the spoon bread recipe which was published in this column in May. Due to the number of requests we will run it again.

Two cups boiling water, 1 cup yellow cornmeal, 1 tablespoon butter, 1½ teaspoons salt, 4 eggs, ½ cup milk, ½ cup flour, 2 tablespoons baking powder, 2 tablespoons sugar.

Gradually add cornmeal to boiling water. Stir in butter and salt and cook over hot water (double boiler) until thick. Then pour mixture into mixing bowl to cool. Meanwhile separate the eggs and beat yolks and milk together, using a rotary beater. When cornmeal mixture is cool beat in the milk mixture. Then add the flour, sugar, and baking powder which you have sifted together. Fold in stiffly beaten egg whites. Pour into well-greased baking dish, about half full, and bake in hot oven 30 to 35 minutes.

SAUCE WITH HARD COOKED EGGS.

We had a waiter in Rector's, an Italian named Giolito, who not only was a fine waiter but knew a good deal about the kitchen. He served me some hard cooked eggs one evening that made a hit. I mean the sauce that went with them, and this is how he did it: Slice lengthwise four hard cooked eggs. Place on top of a slice of tomato one-half of a pimiento and on top of the pimiento the egg. Now on top of each egg place two anchovies crosswise. The sauce was made by adding to ½-cup of catsup 3 tablespoons of olive oil, 1 small button of garlic, and 1 tablespoon of finely chopped parsley, all mixed together, of course, and then poured over the eggs.

ROBERT SAUCE.

Fry a minced onion in a very little fresh butter until it is light yellow, not in the least brown. Add ½ cup brown sauce, slightly diluted with stock. Add a little pepper. Let simmer and add 1 tablespoon vinegar. Just before removing from the stove add 1 tablespoon mustard moistened with vinegar. The mustard should not cook in it.

August 19, 1938

Since mechanical refrigerators are so widely used recipes have to be rewritten for the housewife to obtain maximum efficiency from this most modern of kitchen gadgets. We take as a matter of course a bountiful supply of ice cubes today, but a generation ago this ultra-bit of chic could be had only in the best places.

Rector's was the first restaurant to serve symmetrical ice cubes in beverages. This idea doesn't cause any comment or notice whatsoever but in those good old days it was a novelty and something to write home to the folks about. We prided ourselves as pioneers in many of the niceties of service and fortunately our attention focused on ice. We abhorred the idea of nondescript pieces of ice, so decided to do something about it.

Hospitality in the home usually starts with a beverage of some kind and the gracious hostess will see to it that a fair supply of carbonated water and other beverages is on hand to take care of any guest emergency. Handle your supply of bottled waters just as you would fine champagne. By that I mean have them thoroughly chilled before opening, as this will insure longer effervescence in the beverage. I have been crusading for more years than I care to admit for chilled bottled waters, and as simple as it is, it is amazing how few places serve them this way. After

I offer what I think is constructive criticism against this practice the most plausible excuse that is offered is, "lack of space in the refrigerator."

TWO SUMMER DISHES CHILDREN WILL LIKE.
Oh, well, the proverbial first hundred years are the hardest so let's get on with our recipes. Here is one the children will enjoy:

Refrigerator Ice Cream (Vanilla).
One pint milk, 3 tablespoons cornstarch, ¾ cup sugar, ⅛ teaspoon salt, 2 egg yolks, well beaten, ½ pint heavy cream, 1 teaspoon vanilla.

Dissolve the cornstarch with five tablespoons of cold milk. Put balance of milk in saucepan; stir in cornstarch and beat to boiling point, stirring constantly. Remove from fire; stir in sugar, salt, and well-beaten egg yolks. Let mixture cool, then pour in heavy cream and vanilla and stir until evenly mixed. Pour into refrigerator tray and let freeze in chilling unit for two hours. Remove tray, empty contents into large mixing bowl and beat with a rotary beater for about five minutes to break the ice crystals. Pour mixture back into tray and freeze for one hour. Return mixture to bowl and beat again for five minutes. Pour back into chilling tray and freeze for two hours. It is now ready to serve, but if you wish, you can hold it in the chilling unit for several hours longer.

Here is another recipe that the kiddies will adore:

Frozen Eggnog.
Three eggs, ¼ cup sugar, 1 teaspoon vanilla, few grains salt, ½ pint heavy cream, whipped nutmeg.

Beat eggs and gradually add sugar. Add vanilla and salt and fold in whipped cream. Pour into tray and freeze in chilling unit for about one hour or until partially frozen.

Then stir mixture with a spoon (you can do this right in the tray) and freeze until time of service. This usually requires about three hours. Serve with a slight grating of nutmeg over the top. The old eggnog bowl as I recall it always had sherry for floating, so if you would like a variation in this dessert, substitute three tablespoons of sherry wine for the vanilla.

RECIPE FOR A GLORIFIED BREAD PUDDING.
Now here is a recipe which is somewhat glorified for a bread pudding, but I am sure that you will enjoy having it in your files:

Frozen Bread Pudding.
One cup sugar, 1 cup water, 4 eggs, separated, 1 tablespoon gelatin, 1 cup stale bread crumbs, ½ cup seedless raisins, ½ cup candied fruit, chopped, ½ cup heavy cream flavoring, grated walnuts.

Make a sirup by boiling sugar and water together for five minutes. Meanwhile, beat egg yolks until thick. Now gradually pour sirup onto egg yolks, beating constantly. Pour into top part of double boiler and cook until thick. Then add gelatin which has been softened in three tablespoons of cold water. Let mixture cool; add bread crumbs (all crusts removed) and fruit, then fold it stiffly beaten egg whites and whipped cream which has been flavored to suit your taste. Vanilla, sherry or rum can be used in this recipe. If it is vanilla flavoring you decide on, add one teaspoonful. If sherry or rum add two tablespoons. Fill individual fancy paper cups with the mixture. Sprinkle top with finely grated walnuts and put the cups in the refrigerator tray to freeze for several hours.

August 26, 1938

There are many appetizing odors which assail our nostrils from time to time when good food is being cooked, but the most provokingly nice one is that of bubbling vinegar, spices, and herbs.

Bread baking in the oven is a runner-up and whether the odor permeates the house or is wafted to us on the breeze it is most pleasing to the olfactory nerves.

Many times in my life I have been in farmhouse kitchens, city kitchens, too, watching the procedure of preserving and pickling delectable relishes, and since this is the subject that I started out to tell you about, I had better get started.

There are a great many good recipes for corn relish, all differing just a little from the others. Don't let that confuse you and when you get a recipe from a reliable source experiment with it. Here are a few suggestions that might help you make corn relish to suit your taste. Red cabbage may be used instead of white cabbage. Hot peppers may be used instead of sweet peppers. A combination of red and green peppers may be used instead of just green peppers which so many recipes call for. Ground mustard or mustard seed may be used in the recipe. Instead of using the full amount of cabbage that the recipe calls for use half cabbage and half finely chopped celery, omitting celery seed if that has been written into the recipe. Here is a recipe I think you will like:

CORN RELISH.

Two quarts corn, cut from cob, 2 green sweet peppers, 2 red sweet peppers, 3 pints white cabbage, finely chopped; 1 pound sugar, 4 tablespoons salt, 2 teaspoons celery seed, 2 tablespoons mustard, 3 pints white vinegar.

Select sweet tender corn. With a sharp knife remove kernels, scraping the ears to extract milk and small bits. Wash, seed and chop the peppers finely. Chop cabbage fine by forcing it through the food chopper. Mix all ingredients together, bring slowly to boiling point and cook until corn is soft, which will take 25 to 30 minutes. Put into hot sterilized jars and seal airtight at once.

TOMATO RELISH (UNCOOKED).

One peck ripe tomatoes, 1 pint celery, finely chopped ; 1 pint onions, finely chopped; 3 red peppers, finely chopped; 3 cups sugar, 1 cup salt, ½ cup celery seed, 2 teaspoons cinnamon, 2 teaspoons cloves, 2 teaspoons ground mace, 2 teaspoons white pepper, 3 pints vinegar.

Wash tomatoes; remove stem end and chop fine. Discard celery leaves and finely chop the stalks. Remove all seeds from peppers and chop finely. Drain the chopped tomatoes of all juice and put them in a stone crock. Add balance of ingredients to tomatoes and mix thoroughly. Cover crock and keep in a cool, dry place. Use as wanted.

September is such a bountiful month for fruits and vegetables that it would seem a shame not to preserve a few for later on.

GREEN TOMATO PICKLE

One-half peck tomatoes, thinly sliced, 1 quart onions, thinly sliced, 1 cup salt, 4 sweet peppers (red and green), vinegar, 12 whole cloves, ¼ cup stick cinnamon, 1 teaspoon allspice (tied in spice bag), 3 cups brown sugar, 2 tablespoons celery seed, 2 tablespoons mustard seed.

Put thinly sliced tomatoes and onions in a crock; sprinkle with salt and let stand overnight. In the morning drain and add finely chopped peppers. Start tomatoes, onions, and peppers to cook with just enough vinegar to cover and spice bag. Bring to boiling point and let cook about 30 minutes or until vegetables are soft. Remove spice bag; add sugar, celery, and mustard seed and cook eight or ten minutes longer. Put into hot sterilized jars and seal at once.

Here is a recipe given to me years ago by one of my old cooks.

PICKLED CRAB APPLES.

One-half peck crab apples, 5 cups vinegar, 2 cups water, 5 cups sugar, 1 tablespoon salt, 2 tablespoons whole mixed spices.

Select large crab apples. Wash; do not remove stems. Steam until soft, but do not overcook. Meanwhile, prepare the sirup by boiling together for 10 minutes the vinegar, water, sugar, salt, and spices. Also have ready sterilized jars and caps. Lift crab apples from the steamer by the stems and carefully pack them in the hot sterilized jars. Pour hot spiced sirup over the crab apples, filling the jar to overflowing. Seal at once.

Here is another dandy pickled fruit to grace the dinner table when the roast is being served.

SWEET PICKLED PEARS.

Four pounds pears, whole cloves (about 16), 4 cups sugar (white or brown), 4 pieces stick cinnamon (2 inches long), 3 cups vinegar.

Carefully peel pears, leaving the stems intact. Scoop out blossom end and insert one whole clove. In the meanwhile, prepare the sirup by boiling together for 10 minutes the sugar, vinegar, and cinnamon. Put pears in the sirup and simmer until tender. Lift pears out of sirup and arrange them carefully in hot sterilized jars. Boil sirup 10 minutes longer, then pour it over the fruit filling the jars to overflowing. Seal at once.

September 2, 1938

Labor Day officially spells finis to vacations and summer holidays. For some reason or other appetites seem to change about this time of the year for the more substantial fare. I mean by that, foods that men can put their teeth in, and that, by the way, is right in line with a number of requests for recipes which I have received from the male members of the family.

Marinated beef seems to be right up on top for popularity, so I think we will start off with this European ancestry:

Purchase five to six pounds of beef (top chuck, sirloin or round) and have it cut about three inches thick instead of a chunky piece. Make a marinade as follows:

One pint of red wine vinegar, 1 pint of water, 2 bay leaves, about 10 black peppercorns, 1 medium-sized onion cut in half and studded with several cloves and a blade or two of mace. Bring vinegar, water, and spices to boiling point. Remove from fire; add 1 teaspoon salt and let cool.

Meanwhile rub surface of meat with sugar, using about one-half cupful, and lay it in an earthen dish or stone crock. Pour spiced marinade over the beef and let stand in a cool place or in the refrigerator for two days. Turn the meat several times during the pickling process. Then remove the beef from the marinade, wipe it dry and cover with a light sifting flour. Sear it on all sides in a hot pot roasting kettle in which you have rendered enough fat salt pork to keep it from sticking to the pan. When the meat is browned on all sides, add 1 cupful of the spiced marinade, being sure to corral the onion, 1 bay leaf and half the peppercorns. Lay a slice or two of salt pork on top of the meat; cover pot tightly and pot roast until tender.

This usually takes about two and one-half hours, but the time must always depend on the cut of meat. Turn the meat once or twice during the cooking and, if necessary, add a little of the spiced marinade from time to time. When the meat is cooked remove it to a hot platter while you make the gravy. Remove as much fat from surface as possible. Thicken balance with browned flour; bring to boiling point and strain. If gravy is not sour enough some marinade may be added to it, or at this point a cupful of thick sour cream may be stirred into the hot strained gravy.

EGG NOODLES OR POTATO PANCAKES WITH THIS.

A natural for this tasty dish is to serve egg noodles or potato pancakes. I assume you all know how to prepare noodles and the only bit I'll offer here is to remind you to have them well drained, very hot and tossed with fresh creamery butter. If you want to dress them up a little and make them look pretty, sprinkle a light coating of buttered bread crumbs, which have been fried to a golden brown, over the top.

Now for the potato pancakes to go with our marinated beef. But let me tell you that these pancakes can also be served for a luncheon repast without meat. When they appear in that role they are usually served with fresh, warm applesauce discreetly spiced with cinnamon; or a tart fruit jelly, such as currant. Now for the recipe:

Two cups raw potatoes, coarsely grated, 2 eggs, well beaten, 2 tablespoons flour, 1 teaspoon baking powder, 1 teaspoon salt.

Peel potatoes and let freshen in cold water before grating. Grate potatoes into mixing bowl; add well-beaten eggs and mix thoroughly. Stir in flour, baking powder and salt, which have been sifted together. Drop by spoonfuls onto a hot, well-greased griddle or heavy iron skillet. Bake slowly, and brown on both sides, turning the pancakes but once.

POTATO CROQUETTES FOR A CHANGE.

There are ever so many different ways to prepare potatoes, yet most housewives find themselves resorting to so few ways. How about potato croquettes once in a while? I'll bet you haven't done them in a long time. Well, here's the recipe:

Two cups hot potatoes riced, 2 tablespoons butter, 2 egg yolks, ½ teaspoon salt, ⅛ teaspoon pepper, slight grating of onion (optional).

Mix and beat all ingredients together. Shape into croquettes and dip in fine bread crumbs, then in slightly beaten egg and again in crumbs. Fry in deep hot fat until nicely browned. Fat should be hot enough to brown a one-inch cube of bread in one minute. Drain on unglazed paper and serve hot.

BOILED DINNER OF CORNED BEEF.

Another meat dish that hungry men long for is a boiled dinner of corned beef. When a variety of boiled vegetables is served with corned beef it is known as a New England Boiled Dinner. Here's the recipe and remember to use it when appetites crave a change:

Select a nice piece of corned beef, the cut depending on individual choice. If lean beef is desired, purchase the rump. If a little fat is liked then I would suggest the brisket. Personally I like the brisket or plate. Put the corned beef in a large kettle and cover with cold water. Bring slowly to boiling point and remove scum that rises to the top. Cook over low heat at simmering point until beef is tender. A five-pound piece of beef should simmer for five hours to be perfectly tender.

When cooked remove the meat to a warm dish and skim the water of all fat and cook the various vegetables (cabbage, turnips, carrots, potatoes) in the water in which the meat was cooked. If the turnips, carrots, and potatoes are small, which is preferable, they need not be cut; otherwise cut them into pieces. The head of cabbage is to cut into quarters or eighths.

Boiled beets are included in this dinner, but these are cooked separately in another saucepan. Start them well in advance of the other vegetables, as they require from forty-five minutes to one hour to cook. When vegetables are cooked arrange them in groups around the corned beef which you have placed on a large platter. The beets and cabbage are to be served from separate dishes. Dress cabbage and beets with melted butter, using three parts melted butter to one part vinegar.

NICE VARIATION IN A SAUCE.

Here is a nice variation to serve with the corned beef instead of plain mustard. Also good on baked ham or tongue.

One tablespoon dry mustard, 1 teaspoon powdered sugar, 2 tablespoons vinegar, ¾ cup cream sauce.

Dissolve dry mustard and powdered sugar in the vinegar. Make the cream sauce of medium consistency and while the sauce is hot stir it in gradually to the dissolved ingredients. This mustard sauce should be kept hot in the top part of a double boiler.

September 9, 1938

Now that the months minus the "R" have passed, our thoughts should fondly turn to oysters. From April to September seems a long time for us to deny ourselves the pleasure of eating this delightful sea food that lends itself to innumerable combinations and ways of cookery.

It is impossible to say to whom the honor is due to having established the first oyster house. Without doubt the pioneers in the business were Yankees and the first places of the kind were opened in the great sea coast cities such as New York, Boston, or Baltimore. The further one goes away from the coast the more difficult is the problem of sea food.

However, in 1884 my father conceived the idea that Chicago would welcome an oyster house and backed his judgment by opening one on Clark and Monroe Streets. Three years later the business had so increased that double the floor space had to be taken. Fittings and furnishings were all renewed and the best evidence that these efforts were appreciated was the fact that the patronage of Rector's Oyster House continued to grow apace.

Chicagoans must have been grateful for fresh sea food, for soon after we obtained the privilege of operating a restaurant inside the World's Fair grounds in 1893. This restaurant was known as Cafe Marine, and its specialties were the treasures gleaned from the ocean and fishing banks. There probably was no restaurant in America that went in for more shellfish and sea food specialties than Rector's of Chicago.

There are ever so many ways to prepare oysters and my files are full of recipes, so from time to time we will publish a few good ones.

OYSTERS POULETTE.

Twelve oysters and liquor, 1 cup of cream sauce, few grains cayenne, salt, nutmeg, 2 egg yolks, 2 tablespoons heavy cream, 1 teaspoon strained lemon juice, ¼ cup sliced cooked mushrooms.

Poach the oysters in their own liquor for five minutes or until the edges curl. Remove oysters to hot serving dish. Cook oyster liquor over brisk fire until it is reduced to one-half cup. Then stir in cream sauce and seasonings and bring to a boil. Remove from fire and add the well-beaten egg yolks, cream, lemon juice, and cooked mushrooms. Pour sauce over poached oysters and serve.

OYSTERS AU GRATIN.

One tablespoon diced pimento, grated cheese, 2 tablespoons diced green pepper, 1 cup cream sauce, 12 oysters and liquor.

Poach the oysters in their own liquor for five minutes. Have about one-half cup of liquor in the pan when this is accomplished. Stir in cream sauce which has been seasoned with salt and cayenne pepper. Add green peppers which have been cut into one-quarter-inch dice and blanched for three minutes. Also add the pimentos, which are cut into one-quarter-inch dice. Pour into baking dish, sprinkle grated American, Swiss, or Parmesan cheese over the top, dot with butter, and place in moderate oven to brown.

DOUBLE-DECKER OYSTER PIE.

One quart oysters, 2 cups cracker meal, 1 cup stale bread crumbs, ¾ cup melted butter, ¼ cup cream, salt and pepper.

Prepare a buttered crumb mixture by mixing together cracker meal, bread crumbs, and melted butter. Spread one-third of the mixture in the bottom of a shallow baking dish. Put one-half of the oysters (drained of their liquor) on top and season with a little salt and pepper and pour half the cream over the oysters. Now another layer of buttered crumbs, oysters, seasoning, and cream, and use remaining crumbs to cover the top. Bake in moderately hot oven 25 to 30 minutes.

PIGS IN BLANKETS.

This is a tidy little number to nibble on. Fine at a cocktail party or bridge, especially if the cards have been running right. Cut thinly sliced bacon into lengths that will wrap around the oyster. You will have to decide how many to prepare. Wrap the oysters in the bacon, fastening together with a wooden skewer or toothpick. Lay them on the broiler, and cook in a hot oven until bacon is crisp. If you put them under the broiler flame turn them once for thorough cooking. If you put the pan in the oven no turning is necessary, as heat will strike all sides.

BROILED OYSTERS, CABBAGE RELISH.

Drain oysters of their liquor and roll in finely grated stale bread crumbs. Put them in a double wire broiler, baste with melted butter, and broil under moderate heat until browned, turning once during the cooking. Serve with triangles of freshly made toast and relish.

Cabbage Relish.

Two cups cabbage, finely chopped; 1 cup green pepper, finely chopped; 1 teaspoon celery seed, ½ teaspoon salt, 3 tablespoons sugar, and ⅓ cup vinegar.

Finely chop the cabbage, likewise the green pepper, discarding the seeds and white pulpy part. Add celery seed, salt, sugar, and vinegar. Mix thoroughly and serve.

OYSTER AND SCALLOP FRICASSEE.

If the scallops are small they need not be cut, otherwise cut them in halves or quarters. To 1 cup of scallops add 1 dozen oysters; bring to boil in the strained oyster liquor and let boil for three minutes. Remove oysters and scallops from pan and add thin cream to the liquor to make 2 cupfuls. In another saucepan melt 2 tablespoons of butter and blend in 2 tablespoons of flour. Now pour the hot cream and oyster liquor into the blended butter and flour, stirring constantly until smooth and boiling point is reached. Season with salt and a few grains of cayenne pepper. Add the oysters and scallops, also ½ cup of thinly sliced, cooked mushrooms. Heat thoroughly and just before serving stir in 2 well-beaten egg yolks. Serve in patty shells or in a border of plain boiled rice.

COCKTAIL SAUCE (SHELLFISH).

Now if you would fancy your oysters on the half shell here is a dandy cocktail sauce to serve with them:

Three-quarter cup tomato catsup, ¼ cup grated horseradish, 1 tablespoon Worcestershire sauce, 2 tablespoons lemon juice (strained), 10 drops tabasco sauce, and ¼ teaspoon salt. Mix ingredients and serve in small cocktail glasses.

RUSSIAN COCKTAIL SAUCE.

Same ingredients as above. Add ½ cup of mayonnaise and stir until thoroughly blended. This is especially nice on lobster or crabmeat cocktail.

September 16, 1938

Last week I wrote something about cooking odors, but I forgot to mention a little story that was going the rounds during the Gay Nineties.

There was in those days a popular minstrel troupe traveling all over the country named Thatcher, Primrose and West. The curtain rises and one of the end men opens up with this question: "Mr. Interlocutor, what is the first thing that smells when you go into a drugstore?" Now, back comes the interlocutor and repeats the question. "Well, Mr. Bones, what is the first thing that smells when you go into a drugstore?" The answer is your nose. The gag always got a hearty laugh, and now you have a sample of the humor of the Gay Nineties.

Suppose as of today we put the same question to ourselves. What is the first thing that smells when you go into a drugstore? All right, now get ready for the 1938 answer. Here, it is: Corned beef hash or hamburger steak. Am I right?

The food department of drugstores, as we see it today, no doubt, is very profitable. I find myself occasionally up on a stool eating a sandwich along with a cup of coffee; but the last time I ate in a drugstore I did observe something that got me a little jittery. To the right of me was a huge display of bicarbonate of soda and to the left was a neat pyramid of bottles labeled "citrate of magnesia." Oh, well, what's the difference. Nobody seems to mind and the customers are back just the same, and so am I.

When I was a youngster back in Chicago a chap named Malachy Hogan ran a saloon and lunch counter on Clark Street. At the time, a well-known monologist and comedian, John Kelly, also known as "The Rolling Mill Man," was appearing at one of the vaudeville houses. One night after Kelly finished his act an old friend dropped in and suggested that they go over to Hogan's place for a drink and a bite to eat. The idea pleased Kelly and he gladly accepted the invitation.

Now Hogan's was noted for the genuine limburger cheese with the real tang to it. The friend acted as host and anxious to give Kelly a treat ordered beer and two limburger cheese sandwiches. Kelly took one bite and collapsed. His friend helped him to his feet and wondered what had happened. He assured Kelly that it was only limburger cheese that he started to eat. "Oh, I know it's limburger cheese," replied Kelly, "but what did he put on it?"

Well, now, I think I had better get down to business and few recipes which I hope you will enjoy.

BOILED MUTTON, CAPER SAUCE.

Select the leg or shoulder for this recipe. Have the butcher trim and prepare meat for boiling. Put meat in a large kettle, add one bay leaf, one onion and two slices of lemon. Cover with boiling water; boil hard for eight or ten minutes, and skim. Cover kettle and let meat simmer until tender, allowing thirty minutes to the pound. When meat is half cooked add one teaspoon of salt to water. Let meat drain for five minutes then transfer to a dry, hot platter for service.

Caper Sauce: Melt three tablespoons of butter, blend in three tablespoons of flour, one-half teaspoon of salt and one-eighth teaspoon of pepper. Gradually add one and one-half cups of hot mutton stock which has been skimmed of all fat and strained. Let boil five minutes; remove from fire and add two tablespoons of butter broken into small bits and one-half cup of capers, drained of their liquor and moistened with one teaspoon of strained lemon juice. A nice accompaniment to this dish is mashed turnips.

Not every one is fond of capers, so if you would like something different I would suggest an onion sauce to serve with the boiled mutton.

ONION SAUCE.

Three tablespoons butter, 3 tablespoons flour, 1½ cups hot mutton stock, salt and pepper to taste, 2 tablespoons butter, and 4 medium onions.

Melt butter; blend in flour and gradually add hot mutton stock which has been strained and skimmed of all fat. Season to taste with salt and pepper. Remove from fire and stir in two tablespoons of butter and onions boiled until soft, strained and chopped finely.

Here is a recipe that will take care of the mutton stock which you have on hand; also using the scrag ends of cooked mutton:

SCOTCH BROTH.

Two quarts mutton stock, ¼ cup pearl barley, ¼ cup onion, ½ cup carrots, ½ cup celery, ½ cup white turnips (small diced onion, carrots, celery, turnips), 1 cup shredded cabbage, ¾ cup mutton cut in small pieces or diced, 1 tablespoon finely chopped parsley.

Skim mutton stock of fat, bring to boiling point, and add barley which has been washed in cold water. Add the diced vegetables and shredded cabbage. Cover kettle and let simmer about two hours, stirring occasionally and skimming as necessary. Then add the cooked mutton trimmed of all fat and bone. Serve piping hot with finely chopped parsley sprinkled on top. Soup should be thick, but if it is found to be too thick dilute it with a little stock or water.

SOUTH DOWN SHORTCAKE.

Two cups diced cooked mutton or lamb, 2 chopped hard-cooked eggs, 2 cups rich white sauce, baking-powder biscuits.

Trim meat of all fat and bone and cut in small dice. Combine meat and coarsely chopped eggs with rich white sauce of medium consistency. Serve on freshly baked baking-powder biscuits, lightly buttered.

I have had quite a few requests for German pancakes. Here is the recipe:

GERMAN PANCAKES.

Three eggs, ¾ cup flour, ½ teaspoon salt, 1 tablespoon melted butter, ¾ cup milk.

Beat eggs without separating; add the flour and salt and part of the milk and beat until batter is smooth. Add balance of milk and melted butter. Pour batter into a large well-greased frying pan and bake in a hot oven about 20 minutes. The ideal frying pan for this purpose should be heavy with slightly curved sides. Remove pancake to large hot platter, sprinkle liberally with powdered sugar and cinnamon, and squeeze the juice of half a lemon over all. Roll pancake and serve. Or the pancake may be rolled with jelly or wild cranberries which make a delicious filling. Wild cranberries are very small and are exported to us from Europe.

September 23, 1938

A narrow body of water known as the English Channel separates England from France. The distance is only 20 miles from Calais to Dover, yet the two countries might well be thousands of miles apart as far as habits of eating and drinking go. The Briton likes his food served au naturel, meaning devoid of frills and furbelows, and laughs heartily at the Gaul's system of flavoring the daily provender.

No Parisian would dream seasoning a dish after it arrives at the table, for that would be an insult to the chef. The Englishman, however, surrounds himself with a battery of bottles containing various meat sauces, condiments and prepared mustard and forthwith flavors the dish to suit himself.

The famous Simpson's on the Strand is noted for large joints which are roasted on a dangling spit—roast beef and the ever-popular Southdown mutton with thick broiled chops and steaks running a close second. The climate of England calls for heavy roasts and broils, with solid variations like steak and kidney pies. When the roast or fowl is placed on the table our British cousin starts reaching for the bottles and the first liberal helping is mustard, and, believe me, it's good and hot.

This reminds me of a question that was put to the head of a large mustard concern. He was asked, "How's business?" His reply was, "Excellent," and that brought the comment from the interviewer that people certainly consume a great quantity of mustard. The mustard monarch replied, "Our profits do not come entirely from the amount of mustard that people eat, but rather from what they don't eat."

That's true, I believe, because many a time in Rector's I have seen this happen. The patron will invariably leave on his plate about half of what he has taken.

And so the Englishman must have his mustard to go with his roasts and steaks; but wait, that's not all. He will at the same time help himself to some of the other hot meat sauces such as Worcestershire, walnut ketchup, mushroom ketchup and perhaps several others. Oh, yes, the Englishman has his sauces all right, but not in the manner the Frenchman has them.

In France most dishes are prepared in a sauce. If it's steak, well, that might appear a la Bordelaise, and it's so with fish and vegetables.

The national non-alcohol beverage in England is tea, and their neighbor across the channel goes in for coffee or chocolate. While the Frenchman is drinking his glass of red wine the Englishman is having his half and half or Scotch and soda. That's the difference between two countries which are but 20 miles apart.

FAMILY FAVORITE AND FOR GUESTS, TOO. Now here's a recipe which should become a family favorite. My guess is that company will enjoy it, too:

Onion Soup Au Gratin—Three pints beef stock or consommé, 4 large onions, 3 tablespoons butter, 1 teaspoon Worcestershire sauce, ½ teaspoon salt, ½ teaspoon paprika,

⅛ teaspoon pepper, 2 club rolls, sliced thin, toasted, grated Parmesan cheese.

Slice onions thin and brown in butter. Add more butter if necessary to keep them moist while cooking. When onions are tender add the beef stock, Worcestershire and seasonings. Bring to boiling point; pour soup into earthen or glass casserole (individual size best) and arrange the thinly sliced toaster roll on top. Sprinkle grated Parmesan cheese over roll and put under low broiler flame to brown. A marmite is the proper utensil to serve this type of soup in for a decidedly bourgeois effect.

A broiled halibut steak spread with maitre d'hotel butter offers a change. Would you like to try it?

BROILED HALIBUT, MAITRE D'HOTEL.

Purchase chicken halibut steaks weighing about 12 ounces each. Season with salt and pepper and rub with soft butter. Place on greased rack of broiler under moderate flame until nicely browned, allowing about 8 minutes to each side. Remove steak to hot platter and spread with maitre d'hotel butter made as follows: Cream 3 tablespoons of butter. Add a light pinch of cayenne pepper, one teaspoon of finely chopped parsley and 1 teaspoon of strained lemon juice. A supply of this butter should be kept in the refrigerator. Excellent on grilled steak and fish.

Small fish or fillets of fish when sautéed in the frying pan to a golden brown (known to the French as dores or gilded) are sautéed in clarified butter to a light golden brown and served as a dry sauté. Here is an example:

FILLET OF SOLE, DOREE.

Since we do not have sole in our local waters we use the nearest fish resembling it, which is flounder. Flounder fillets may be purchased the year around and from coast to coast. Season fillets with salt and white pepper and dip lightly in flour. Fry in clarified butter to a light golden brown. Remove to hot platter or plate and serve with half a lemon. Garnish with a sprig of parsley.

Now if we fancy a sauté Meuniere we proceed as above and when the fish is transferred to a hot plate it is sprinkled with finely chopped parsley and a few drops of lemon juice. A piece of butter is then put in the frying pan and when it turns to a light brown it is immediately removed from the fire and poured over the fish. Allow one tablespoon of golden-brown butter for each service. This a la Meuniere mode is also suited to the preparation of frogs' legs, sweetbreads, trout, shad roe, calves' liver all small fish, or fish fillets.

VEGETABLE PANACHE.

The next recipe which I will give you is a delectable one for the serving of fresh green vegetables. It is called "Panache."

This is a combination of three fresh green vegetables and was a specialty of Rector's Restaurant. Combine equal portions of new string beans, cut en Julienne, new lima beans, and new green peas which have been cooked separately in boiling salted water. When vegetables are tender they are thoroughly drained of all water and lightly seasoned with salt and white pepper. They are then arranged in three distinct layers in a large vegetable dish and whipped cream covers the entire top. In serving use a large spoon and cut through the whipped cream right down to the bottom layer of vegetables. This is good. However, just another word. Do not whip cream too stiff—just enough to hold its shape and seep through the vegetables.

September 30, 1938

It's fun to be in a business that ties in with one's hobby and that is just what I have been doing for the last 40 years. There are some people whom I have met that don't seem at all interested in good food. They have no palate and food flavors mean nothing at all. They just go on eating to keep the machinery working and regard food as fuel and nothing more.

No two men who ever came into Rector's—and they dined there together nightly—got more real enjoyment and pleasure out of their food than the late Charles Frohman and Charles Dillingham. It just seemed as if they anticipated their evening meal with delight. Of course, we had hundreds of different foods which came out of the kitchen, but these two gentlemen never tired of one of our specialties and that was Crabmeat Mornay.

By actual count they started their dinner with Crabmeat Mornay and made that a standing order for 30 days. The Mornay part is the sauce and the sauce is a combination of rich cream sauce, two kinds of grated cheese—Swiss and Parmesan—butter and seasonings.

I suppose when one gets right down to the fundamental points of cookery, especially in the preparation of sauces, it can be likened to chemistry. Those crack chefs that I met and worked with in Paris were continually experimenting with combination of foods in search of a new flavor—something different.

LIKED BY ARMY MEN ON TROPICAL ISLAND.

The other day I was talking to Steve Hannigan, who appreciates and knows good food. He took from his pocket several recipes which he explained were outstanding native foods in San Juan, Puerto Rico. American Army officers and their wives stationed on this tropical island are as fond of curry for a hot-weather dish as are the British officers in India and China.

The head chef at the Ballaja officer's club of the Sixty-fifth United States Infantry Regiment has a special recipe for chicken curry with which to tempt the guests who gather in the garden of ancient El Morro fortress for buffet suppers. The side dish he recommends is his own recipe for a carrot mold. And for a cold dessert an exotic Spanish dish known as "Bien Me Sabe."

CHICKEN CURRY.

Three pounds chicken, cut in pieces, ⅓ cup butter, 2 onions, chopped fine, 2 teaspoons salt, 1 teaspoon vinegar, 1 tablespoon sugar, 1½ tablespoons curry powder, flour.

Melt butter in hot saucepan, add chicken and cook 10 minutes. Add liver and heart and cook another 10 minutes. Add onion, salt, vinegar, sugar, and curry powder. Cover with boiling water and simmer until chicken is tender. Remove chicken and strain liquor. Measure, and thicken with one tablespoon of flour to each cup of liquid. Mix with enough cold water to make it pour easily. Pour over chicken and simmer again. Serve in border of boiled rice. Garnish with green and red pepper, finely minced, and grated coconut. Serve chopped peanuts, mango, and chutney on the side.

CARROT MOLD.

Four cups mashed boiled carrots, 1 cup cracker crumbs, 3 eggs, ¼ pound butter, salt and pepper to taste.

Mix the carrots and cracker crumbs, and well-beaten eggs, and spread half the mixture on the bottom and sides of the mold. Place two cups of spinach or baby peas in the center. Cover with the remainder of the carrot mixture. Steam for two hours and serve with drawn butter.

Now for the piece de resistance:

BIEN ME SABE.

One coconut, ¼ pound rusk or sponge cake, 1 pound sugar, ⅛ quart sweet wine, 8 egg yolks, 2 sticks cinnamon, ⅛ teaspoon cinnamon.

Grate the coconut, extract the milk, and add the milk to half the water of the coconut. Beat the egg yolks and have them ready. Make a sirup of the coconut milk, sugar and cinnamon sticks. When it is half cooked (about five minutes of cooking), add the egg yolks, beating constantly and keeping the fire low so that they will not over cook or separate. Place the mixture in the refrigerator to chill. Cut the rusk or sponge cake in oblong pieces and place in the bottom of a deep dish. Moisten with the sweet wine. Then cover the cake with the chilled custard and powdered cinnamon. Put back in the refrigerator till ready to serve.

SIMPLE DESSERT EASY TO MAKE.

Now for a simple old-fashioned dessert that is quickly and easily made.

Jelly Roll.

Two eggs, 1 cup sugar, grated rind of 1 lemon, 1 tablespoon melted butter, ⅓ cup hot water, 1 cup pastry flour, 1½ teaspoons baking powder, ⅛ teaspoon salt.

Beat eggs until light, and lemon colored. Add sugar gradually and grated lemon rind, melted butter and hot water. Sift pastry flour, baking powder and salt and fold into first mixture. Line shallow pan with paper, turn in batter and bake in a moderate oven (350 degrees) 20 minutes. Turn out of pan at once onto a clean towel, cut off all four crisp edges, spread with jelly and roll lightly and quickly. Sprinkle top with confectioners' sugar.

STANDARD SUGAR COOKIE RECIPE.

How about filling the cookie jar for the kiddies? Here is the standard sugar cookie recipe:

One cup butter, 2 cups sugar, cup cream, 2 eggs well beaten. ¼ cup cream, 3 ¾ cups flour, 2 teaspoons baking powder, 1 teaspoon flavoring.

Cream the butter and gradually add one-half of the sugar. Add the eggs and continue to beat until light and fluffy. Gradually beat in the remaining sugar. Mix and sift the flour and baking powder and add it to the first mixture, alternating with the cream. Beat the dough well after each addition of flour, as this will ensure a smooth mixture. Add flavoring last or it may be added to the cream. Place the cookie dough in the refrigerator to chill for several hours or over night. Roll the dough on a lightly floured board to about one-eighth of an inch thickness. Sprinkle dough with sugar which should be gently pressed in with the rolling pin. Cut with cookie cutter and bake in hot oven until browned or about 10 minutes. Cookies should be removed from baking sheet while hot to prevent breaking.

October 7, 1938

It is estimated that 50,000,000 people will visit the World's Fair in New York next summer. The preparation and service of food to such a stupendous crowd is particularly interesting to me, so I decided to go out to the Fair grounds and find out all about it.

Lovers of hot dogs and hamburgers—and aren't we all?—need have no fear that their appetites will not be sated, because there will be 30,000,000 pieces of them all ready to dish up. Aside from the hot dog emporiums there will be about 80 restaurants, of which 17 will be foreign. These foreign restaurants will be operated for the most part in connection with the foreign exhibits.

Famous restaurateurs from New York, Chicago and other large cities will be among the concessionaires. Every known type of eating place has been arranged for—cafeterias, lunch counters, tearooms, theater restaurants, swank supper clubs, as well as private clubs and beer pavilions. These restaurants will serve food that will appease the appetites of all. Moderate prices, I am informed, will prevail in most of the restaurants.

Now, all this chatter about eating at the Fair leads up to a bit of news I have been saving for you. I am going to make my headquarters at the gas exhibit, where I will have a perfectly appointed modern kitchen to conduct cooking demonstrations several times daily. Every Rector specialty and many other foods will be prepared before you. It will please me very much to be of service to you in solving any of your cookery problems. So let me, now, in this column, extend a personal invitation to you all to come into my kitchen at the Fair.

OX TAIL EN CASSEROLE SAVORY DISH.

Now that cooler days are here what is nicer to tempt the appetite than a savory casserole? Here is a recipe that I am sure you will use often:

Wash and dry on clean towel 2 oxtails that have been cut into joints. Dredge lightly with flour and brown in large iron frying pan with half butter and beef drippings. When nicely browned on all sides, season with salt, pepper and a liberal amount of paprika. Then add 1 pint of strong beef stock, a bouquet of celery leaves and parsley, 1 bay leaf, a little mace and about 6 whole black peppercorns. Bring up to boiling point, then transfer to covered casserole dish to finish cooking in a moderate oven.

Oxtails require long, slow cooking, so allow 3 or 4 hours in the oven. Add small white onions and carrots to casserole toward the last, allowing 1 hour for them to cook. It will also be necessary to add a little more stock from time to time, as it reduces during the oven cooking. Skim off surface fat, add 1 cupful canned tomato pulp and thicken with browned flour. Serve from casserole dish.

ROAST FRESH HAM, CIDER SAUCE.

Whole fresh ham, 3 cups cider, 2 medium sized onions, sliced; 3 or 4 whole cloves, 1 bay leaf, salt, black pepper, 1 cup fine dry bread crumbs, flour, ¼ cup seeded raisins.

Scrub ham, place rind side up on rack in open roasting pan. Pour over cider, add onions, cloves, and bay leaf. Bake in slow oven (300 degrees), allowing 30 minutes per pound. One hour before ham is done, carefully remove rind. Score fat lightly, season generously with salt and pepper and cover fat with bread crumbs. Remove excess fat from pan drippings. Continue roasting ham 1 hour, but do not baste. Remove ham to large hot platter. Strain liquid and thicken gravy, allowing 1 tablespoon of flour to each cup of liquid. Add raisins, which have been covered with boiling hot water and allowed to stand until cool. Season with salt if necessary.

THREE RECIPES FOR SMALLER CUTS OF MEAT.
Here are several dandy recipes for smaller cuts of meat.

Veal Cutlet Marengo.

One veal cutlet, about 2 pounds, 3 tablespoons fat, 2 tablespoons tomato puree, ½ cup white wine, 2 onions, minced, 1 clove garlic, minced, 2 tablespoons oil, 1 cup canned tomato pulp, 1 teaspoon salt, ½ teaspoon pepper, 1 cup sliced mushrooms.

Wipe veal cutlet with damp cloth. Brown well on both sides in a large frying pan, using half melted veal fat and half butter. When browned add tomato puree and white wine. A dry California wine is inexpensive and will do nicely. In a separate pan sauté the onions and garlic in oil, add tomato pulp, salt and pepper; heat thoroughly and pour over cutlet. Cover pan and simmer slowly for two hours. Just before serving add mushrooms which have been sautéed in butter for several minutes.

Veal Birds.

Use slices about one-half inch thick cut from the leg of veal. Have butcher pound them flat until one quarter inch thick. Cut in pieces two or three inches wide and four or five inches long. Spread each strip with a savory bread stuffing and roll. Wrap each piece with thinly sliced bacon and fasten with toothpicks. To cook the veal birds brown them in a hot pan, then cover pan and cook over low heat or in a moderate oven until the meat is tender—about 45 minutes.

For a variety stuffing you could use a light spreading of liverwurst with fine bread crumbs on top. A well-seasoned tomato sauce goes well with this dish.

Veal Chops à la Zingara.

Four loin veal chops, salt and pepper, melted veal fat, 1 medium-sized onion, chopped; 4 carrots, sliced; 2 tomatoes, ⅓ cup white wine (dry); 1 cup mushrooms, sliced.

Have chops cut about one inch thick. Season with salt and pepper and sear in hot fat until nicely browned. Add onion, carrots, and tomatoes which have been peeled and quartered. Add wine, cover pan and simmer slowly for 45 minutes. Add mushrooms which have been sautéed in butter for several minutes, heat thoroughly and serve.

If fresh mushrooms are not available, canned mushrooms may be used in the recipe. Since canned mushrooms are already cooked they need only to be sliced and added to the dish just long enough in advance to heat thoroughly. The same could apply to fresh tomatoes; if they are not in market, use canned tomatoes.

October 14, 1938

One of my fans living in Denver., Colo., wrote me as follows: "Dear Mr. Rector, I would appreciate it more than I can tell you if you would do me the great favor of answering this letter:

"I cook for a living, and have had the opportunity to cook and prepare many lobsters. This is what I want to know from you as you are considered the finest authority on foods and the preparation of same.

"Yesterday my employer gave me two lobsters to cook. They were supposed to be live ones sent here from the East packed in ice. But they were dead. We are sure of that, because we gave them ample time to recover from the cold, also giving them other methods of trying to revive them, but to no avail. I refused to cook them because I had always been told that as soon lobster dies poison goes into the meat and should not be used.

"What I would like you to tell me, did I do the right thing? I will be deeply grateful if you will take time to answer.

"Yours truly.
"Mrs. A. O."

LOBSTERS NEED NOT BE ALIVE.
I wrote this lady as follows:

Granting that the lobsters that you received were alive when packed in ice for shipment, but appeared lifeless when you unpacked them, this did not indicate that they were unfit for food.

You could have with all safety plunged them into boiling water, boiling them the required length of time, according to weight, and the meat would have been just as good and wholesome to eat as if the lobsters were alive and kicking when received.

Lobsters do die in transit, but if too much time does not elapse, and the lobsters have been kept at fairly even temperature, they are perfectly good to eat.

A great many people are under the same impression as you, but it is a mistaken idea.

I don't believe there was a restaurant either in Chicago or New York that sold more lobsters than we did in Rector's. Our lobster shipper in Boston and in Maine used the utmost care in seeing that our lobsters were alive and also they were properly packed in ice and seaweed. These lobsters arrived in barrels and each one of them was carefully examined. True, we did find perhaps two or three out of the shipment that were not alive, but they were not thrown out. Instead, these lobsters were immediately placed in a large pot to boil and later to be used in salads or reheats such as lobster Newburg.

CRABS AND SHRIMPS ANOTHER STORY.

Never in all the years that we were in the restaurant business did we get one complaint that a customer was "poisoned." Personally, I would not eat any shellfish, which includes hard and soft shell crabs and shrimp, if I knew that they had been dead for some time and had not been kept under proper refrigeration.

Fresh crab meat which is shipped out of Virginia and Maryland in cans (these cans are not hermetically sealed, but the covers are tied on with a piece of white cord), is of course, cooked. When this meat is removed from the crabs it is immediately packed in one-pound cans and the covered cans are packed in ice and promptly shipped out. It is extremely perishable and should not be kept longer than one day. Canned crab meat which is hermetically sealed can be kept on the pantry shelf almost indefinitely.

SEAFOOD NEWBURG A POPULAR DISH.

Every so often there appeared on the menu of Rector's a dish that was very popular. It was known as Seafood Newburg, and consisted of several varieties of shellfish. Here is the recipe:

Seafood Newburg.

Two and one-half cups rich cream sauce, 2 egg yolks, well beaten, 3 cups cooked seafood (crab meat, shrimp, lobster), 2 tablespoons butter, 1 tablespoon sherry, salt and light pinch cayenne pepper.

When cream sauce has reached boiling point remove from fire and slowly blend in egg yolks. Then add seafood (which can be either fresh or canned) butter, sherry and seasonings. Do not allow sauce to boil again, but it can be kept hot by placing saucepan over hot water. Serve with triangles of freshly made toast, or in patty shells. When oysters are in season add six or eight medium-sized ones which have been poached in their own liquor for three minutes. They can be added along with the mixed seafood.

RECIPE FOR OYSTER OMELET.

For Mrs. K. C., who requests a recipe for oyster omelet. It being an unusual recipe, I thought others would like to try it.

Oyster Omelet.

Six eggs, 4 tablespoons milk or water, ½ teaspoon salt, ⅛ teaspoon white pepper, 2 tablespoons butter, 1 cup cream sauce, 1 pint oysters, finely minced parsley.

Beat eggs well with milk, salt and pepper. Melt butter in large omelet pan, tilting the pan so the melted butter will coat the sides of the pan. Pour in eggs and as they begin to set, take a spatula and lift the edges so the uncooked egg can reach the bottom of pan. Use the spatula in this fashion until the top of the omelet is set and bottom of omelet is lightly browned.

In the meanwhile have ready one cup of medium cream sauce and, in a separate saucepan poach the oysters in their own liquor for five minutes. Drain oysters of all liquor and arrange half of them in the middle of the omelet. Carefully fold the omelet over and transfer to a hot platter. Garnish ends of omelet with remaining oysters and pour the cream sauce over oyster garnish. Sprinkle a pinch of finely minced paisley over the oysters which are at either end and serve immediately.

Here is something nice for a Sunday morning breakfast.

Codfish Puffs.

Two cups shredded codfish, 2 cups freshly boiled riced potatoes, 1 tablespoon butter, 1 teaspoon grated onion, 2 eggs, well beaten, ¼ teaspoon white pepper.

Freshen codfish by tying in piece of cheese cloth and squeezing in cold water. Add remaining ingredients and beat with a fork until thoroughly mixed. Drop by spoonfuls into deep hot fat (hot enough to brown a one-inch cube of bread in 60 seconds) until nicely browned. Drain on unglazed paper and serve with special tomato sauce.

Special Tomato Sauce.

One-half cup melted butter, ½ cup chili sauce, ½ cup ketchup.

Melt butter in top part of double boiler; stir in chili sauce and tomato catsup and heat over hot water.

October 21, 1938

Why are there so many women engaged in the restaurant business? That question has been asked of me scores of times. I may or may not have the answer, but first I can state that there are more women restauranteurs than ever before, and they are increasing in numbers each year.

Let's take for example a young woman who has just completed a course in domestic science—and there are many schools and colleges throughout the country offering this course. There are also plenty of restaurants and hotels that are eager to employ trained women in their establishments, which is fine all around, as it enables the school graduate the perfect opportunity to get practical working knowledge of cooking and service.

Many of these young women look forward to the day when they will own their own tea rooms, cafeterias or restaurants. Others are content to remain in the field that employs them to manage experimental kitchens or manage lunch rooms or restaurants of large manufacturing plants, schools and other public institutions, as well as hospitals. All these jobs, I am told, pay good salaries.

UNLIMITED FIELD IN FOOD WORLD.
Young American boys associate the idea of cooking with the fair sex. This is only natural, as the home atmosphere

is founded on these lines, and he is seldom encouraged to learn or assist in any of the family cooking. This situation does not exist in European homes, as boys as well as girls are taught to cook. It is this early training that decides many a young chap on cooking as a profession.

When this decision is made the boy finds himself working in the kitchen of a famous hotel or restaurant, having apprenticed himself to the task for little or no money. This apprenticeship includes training in every department of the kitchen from garde manager to chef-saucier. The next step places the boy or young man as chef in complete charge of a kitchen of perhaps lesser proportions.

The thought that I want to convey is that the field and opportunity for young people in the commercial food world is unlimited, provided you apply yourself in a serious manner. There will always be food and there will always be people, also 365 days in the year, to conjure with, so there must of necessity be cooks.

A CLASSIC IN EGG RECIPES.

It has just occurred to me that we haven't included egg recipes in the column lately, with the exception of the omelet recipe which appeared last week. Here is a classic which has been in the Rector portfolio for years. The first time I saw this dish prepared was when I was serving my apprenticeship in the kitchen of the Cafe de Paris, Paris, France:

EGGS AU BEURRE NOIR
(Black Butter).

Four eggs, 1 tablespoon butter, salt and pepper, 1½ tablespoons butter, 1½ tablespoons vinegar, 1 teaspoon chives, finely chopped.

Melt one tablespoon of butter in small frying pan and cook eggs over low heat until set. Remove to hot plates, taking care not to break the yolks. Season with salt and pepper and sprinkle over with finely chopped chives. Add remaining butter to frying pan, let it turn brown, remove from fire, and add vinegar. Pour over eggs and serve immediately. The vinegar combining with the hot butter makes a delightful sauce for eggs cooked in this manner. If chives are not available you have my permission to scrape a few slivers of garlic over the eggs; but remember, this is off the record, as it isn't strictly a la Rector, but good.

NICE EGG DISH WITH MEAT GARNISH.

Here is a dandy luncheon egg dish, especially nice if garnished with broiled sausages, grilled lamb, or veal kidneys or bacon.

EGG TIMBALE.

Two tablespoons butter, 2 tablespoons flour, 1¼ cups milk, ½ teaspoon salt, ⅛ teaspoon pepper, ⅛ teaspoon celery salt, few grains cayenne pepper, 6 eggs, 2 tablespoons parsley, finely chopped.

Cream the butter, add flour, and pour on gradually scalded milk. Add seasonings and cook in top part of double boiler for five minutes. Separate eggs, beat yolks until thick and lemon colored and add them to the hot milk sauce. Beat egg whites until stiff, then fold them into the egg yolk and milk mixture, along with the finely chopped parsley. Turn mixture into buttered timbale molds, set in pan of hot water (like baked custard) and bake in moderate oven (325 degrees) until firm or about 30 minutes.

EGGS FLORENTINE.

It is nice to serve eggs in this manner in small earthen dishes for individual service. Butter the bottom of each individual dish and then put one-half cup of freshly cooked chopped spinach in each one. Sprinkle one teaspoon of grated Swiss cheese over spinach. Then drop one or two eggs into each dish, taking care not to break the yolks. Cover with rich cream sauce and sprinkle top with grated Swiss cheese. Place in a hot oven until eggs are cooked and top is delicately browned.

Here is a recipe for family dessert:

BROWN BETTY.

Three cups soft bread crumbs, ½ cup melted butter, 3 cups thinly sliced apples, 1 cup sugar, 1 teaspoon cinnamon, grated lemon rind.

Mix bread crumbs with melted butter. Fill baking dish with alternate layers of buttered crumbs and sliced apples, sprinkling each layer of apple with sugar, cinnamon, and grated lemon rind. Have top layer covered with crumbs. Bake about one hour in moderate oven 350 degrees. Uncover dish last 20 minutes to brown top. Serve hot with plain cream. This dessert is delicious when served with hard sauce, try it for a change.

HARD SAUCE.

Three tablespoons brandy, sherry or rum, few grains nutmeg, ½ cup butter, 1 cup powdered sugar.

Cream butter, add sugar gradually, and cream until light and fluffy. Add flavoring drop by drop. Pile lightly in glass dish and sprinkle a few grains of nutmeg over the top.

October 28, 1938

Precisely at 5:30 in the afternoon, when the chef of Rector's came on duty for the evening service, the very first thing he did was to walk over to the Bain-Marie to taste each and every one of the soups. The soups du jour usually consisted of four, and they could be either thick or thin. Among these du jour soups could be Chicken Gumbo, Bisque of Lobster, Minestrone, Clam Chowder, Philadelphia Pepper Pot, etc. There were at all times the two consommés, light and dark, to be served plain or with various garnitures. The consommés—call them as you wish, beef broth or chicken broth—took many hours to make to bring them up to the point of stock.

To my way of thinking, the quality of the stock is the base which is going to make a good soup or a poor soup. After the light or dark stock was clarified we had the base from which many varieties could be developed. Gelatine was never used in Rector's in the preparation of cold consommés. There was no occasion for it.

In making the beef stock there was an overabundance of meat and bones, and so it was in the number of fowl that were boiled to prepare the chicken stock or consommé. Naturally, the stock would, when cooled off and placed in the refrigerator, jell of its own accord.

PERFECT MEAL STARTS WITH GOOD SOUP.

On many occasions I have given my definition of a perfect meal (providing, of course, you do not come to the table with a Rocky Mountain appetite), and it is a goodly quantity of good soup, a salad, a dessert and beverage. Don't you think that rounds out a satisfying meal?

Consommé when garnished with various bits of diced meat, vegetables or royales (egg custard), takes on an interesting character. Consommé should be of good strength, so let's start with that recipe:

CONSOMMÉ.

Three pounds fowl, 3 pounds knuckle of veal, 2 pounds bottom round and marrow bones, 6 quarts cold water, 3 sprigs parsley, 2 sprigs marjoram, 2 sprigs thyme, ½ bay leaf, 3 cloves, 10 peppercorns, 1 tablespoon salt, 1 medium-sized onion, sliced, ½ cup carrots, diced, ½ cup celery and leaves, sliced.

Have fowl drawn but do not cut it up. Cut veal and beef into small pieces. Put whole fowl and veal into soup kettle; cover with cold water and let stand while you prepare the beef. Scrape the marrow from the bones into a hot frying pan, add cut pieces of beef and brown on all sides. Add browned beef and bones to soup kettle and bring very slowly to the boiling point. Reduce heat to minimum and simmer five hours. Add vegetables and seasonings and simmer two hours longer. Strain, cool, remove fat and clear with white of egg before serving. Fowl may be used for chicken salad or sandwiches.

Finely chopped raw lean beef or white of egg is the medium employed for clearing consommé or soup stock. The albumen in either will coagulate the tiny particles, causing them to precipitate to the bottom. Since white of egg is all albumen, we will use that. When consommé has been strained, cooled and all fat removed, the desired quantity is measured into another saucepan. To each quart of cold consommé you will add the white of one egg which has been slightly beaten with one tablespoon of water. Break the shell into small pieces and add that, too. Bring the consommé to boiling point, stirring constantly; let boil for two or three minutes. Remove from fire and let stand for 15 minutes. Strain through double thickness of cheese cloth. Can be served as a clear consommé or a garniture can be added.

VARIETY OF CONSOMME RECIPES.

Now this is what I mean by variety in consommé:

CONSOMMÉ ALFREDO.

Into each plate of hot consommé add one poached egg and sprinkle top with grated Parmesan cheese. Egg must be carefully poached in hot water, then drained and added to consommé.

CONSOMMÉ ROYAL.

The egg custard is to be prepared several hours in advance, as it must be thoroughly cold before cutting into dice. To be made as follows: Slightly beat the yolks of three eggs, add one-third cup of consommé, a few grains of salt and a tiny pinch of nutmeg. Pour into a small buttered baking dish, place in pan of hot water and bake in moderate oven until firm. Cut cold custard into small dice of either one-quarter or one-half inch. The important thing is not the size of the dice but the precision in cutting. Have these small royales as alike as peas and add 8 or 10 to each plate of hot consommé.

Now we will take a top flight into something really good.

CHICKEN GUMBO.

Six cups consommé, ½ cup sliced okra. ½ cup diced chicken (white meat only), ¼ cup diced ham, 1 cup canned tomatoes, ½ cup cooked rice; salt and pepper taste.

Slice okra into one-quarter inch slices. Add to chicken consommé and cook for 20 minutes. Add breast of fowl cut into one-half inch dice, cooked ham cut into smaller dice and canned tomato pulp, which you will shred apart, taking care to discard the seed center. Also add the cooked rice, which is well drained so that each grain stands apart. Bring to the boiling point, add seasonings to taste, and serve.

A chiffonade of lettuce or sorrel can be added to a plain consommé and again we have something delightful and quite out of the ordinary.

CONSOMMÉ ALEXANDRIA.

Wash and thoroughly dry the leaves or sorrel or lettuce. Shred into very fine strips, discarding the center rib section. Bring consommé to boiling point; remove from fire and add the shredded sorrel or lettuce, allowing one tablespoon to each quart of consommé. Let stand 15 or 20 minutes, as the heat of the consommé will sufficiently wilt the tiny shreds without actual cooking. Meanwhile prepare the balance. Set to boil about three tablespoons of tapioca and when cooked and quite clear strain it through a thickness of muslin. Also cut a piece of the breast of fowl into Julienne strips. Now add the fowl and tapioca to the consommé and bring all to just under the boiling point and serve.

November 4, 1938

Of course, we all know that adage about doing a thing the right way or the wrong way. Well, it applies to cookery very definitely. And I have found also that a person who does not like to cook is never going to turn out good things to eat. He or she is hopeless and the sooner and more often they put the can opener to use, the more content they will be.

If you have a liking for cooking and happen to be a beginner, don't let a few failures discourage you. We who write recipes endeavor to present them to you in a simplified manner. Cooking to please everybody all the time is impossible. That I do know after a quarter of a century in Rector's.

POPULAR WAY OF SERVING SPAGHETTI.

There are certain dishes that are known as a whole meal. I have in mind spaghetti, and if you will try the following recipes sometime I am sure you will make a big hit with the family. My only suggestion is, prepare enough!

Of all the different ways of serving spaghetti in Rector's, the recipe I am giving you now was by far the most popular:

SPAGHETTI MILANAISE.

One-half pound spaghetti, 1 can tomatoes (No. 2 size), 1 can tomato sauce, 1 cup stock, ½ teaspoon garlic, minced, ½ teaspoon salt, 1/8 teaspoon pepper, 1 teaspoon paprika, 1 bay leaf, 1 teaspoon Worcestershire sauce, 2 thin slices boiled ham, 6 thin slices boiled tongue, 1 cup mushrooms, thinly sliced, 1 tablespoon butter, grated Parmesan cheese.

Cook spaghetti in large quantity of boiling salted water until tender, or about 10 or 12 minutes. Drain and rinse with cold water. In the meantime prepare the sauce as follows: Simmer together for 20 minutes canned tomatoes, tomato sauce or puree, stock, garlic, salt, pepper, paprika, bay leaf, and Worcestershire. Then add ham and tongue which you have cut in Julienne strips and let simmer 10 minutes longer.

If canned mushrooms arc used they need only be sliced and added along with the ham and tongue, as they are cooked and only need to be thoroughly heated in the sauce. Fresh mushrooms must be thinly sliced and sautéed in a little butter until soft before adding to the sauce.

Add drained spaghetti to the sauce; mix and heat thoroughly and just before serving add the butter and serve. Grated Parmesan cheese is sprinkled liberally over each portion. This is always done at the table, so prepare a good quantity of grated cheese before sitting down.

SPAGHETTI ALFREDO WITH MEAT SAUCE.

Last March we wrote in this column a recipe for spaghetti served with the popular meat sauce. As this particular recipe entails the pot roasting of a piece of beef, it has been worked out on a larger scale using one pound of spaghetti. By request, here it is.

SPAGHETTI ALFREDO.

The actual cooking of spaghetti is easy. All you need is a whole lot of galloping boiling water. Drop in the spaghetti, along with some salt. You can boil it for ten minutes or up to twelve minutes. Italians never cook spaghetti to the soft stage and they have a term they use in regard to this which is "dente." It simply means something to bite with the teeth.

When the spaghetti is cooked it is drained into a colander and hot or cold water is poured over it. It is then ready to combine with the sauce.

Spaghetti without a sauce doesn't make sense. I have eaten spaghetti all over Italy and there's a different sauce for every section. Milan has its way of preparing the sauce; so has Florence and Naples and Genoa. But they all agree on three of the ingredients that go in the sauce and these are olive oil, tomatoes and garlic. You can't dodge them no matter where you go in Italy.

Alfredo of Rome makes his meat sauce by first pot roasting four pounds of lean brisket of beef or the cut you prefer. Put one-third cup of olive oil in a heavy pot or casserole; when the oil is hot sear the meat on all sides. Reduce the heat, and season with salt; add two bay leaves, a pinch of thyme, 12 whole black peppercorns and two buttons of garlic. Now cover the pot or casserole and simmer for two and one-half hours, turning the meat occasionally. Then add a No. 2 size can of tomatoes and cook 30 minutes longer.

When you remove the meat there should be about two cupfuls of liquid remaining. Strain and add to it one cup of tomato sauce or puree. Put the meat through the food chopper and add it and the spaghetti to the sauce. Heat thoroughly and pile the spaghetti on a large hot platter and serve. Sprinkle top liberally with grated Parmesan cheese.

The tomato sauce referred to in the recipes may be purchased in Italian or American grocery stores. It comes in small cans, holding about one cupful of thick sauce.

November 11, 1938

Whenever you are in doubt just what to serve as the main course for dinner on some special occasion I think I can help you out. It's going to cost you some money all right, but, of course, you will be guided by your budget.

The food I have in mind is fillet mignon, and is well liked by man, woman, and child. The fillet which your butcher will point out to you lies inside of a short loin of beef, imbedded in a thick layer of fat. The fillet itself is clear meat from tip to tip and that's one reason why you will pay a top price for it. It is not only the tenderest cut from the steer but the most expensive. A whole fillet varies in weight, but the average, let's say, weighs about 8 pounds.

A whole fillet after it is cooked will serve nicely eight or ten people. If you decide to cook one some time do not fail to have it larded with thin strips of larding pork, and, from this point on, roast it as you would a roast of beef, basting it every 15 minutes. The oven should be medium hot, and allow about one and one-half hours for the roasting. About 45 minutes before the fillet is ready add to the roasting pan 10 or 12 small peeled potatoes, turning them once while roasting, and you will have what is known as rissolee potatoes. A couple of dozen fresh mushrooms could be added, say 10 minutes after the potatoes.

Now for the sauce or gravy. Skim as much of the fat as you can from the small amount of liquid in the pan, and because a fillet is never too juicy, add a small can of consommé to the pan. Let it come to a boil, at the same time loosening all the essence which clings to bottom of pan. Thicken with a little flour dissolved in cold water. Bring to boiling point, season to taste, strain and serve in a separate sauce boat.

There are possibly 100 ways to prepare fillet mignon. Every night there appeared on the menu of Rector's a fillet mignon a la this or a la that. But fillet mignon a la Stanley was very popular because it was somewhat of a novelty to serve a cooked fruit garnish with meat. It was a daring departure from the usual apple sauce with duck or pork or cranberry sauce with the holiday turkey. Fruits are used in great variety today as a meat garnish—every kind from the lowly prune to the glorious white grape.

FILLET MIGNON À LA STANLEY.

Have the butcher cut from a tenderloin of beef slices to weigh five to six ounces apiece. Also have them flattened to one inch thickness by placing in a towel and using the flat side of a cleaver, taking care to shape into rounds during the process. Dip each fillet in melted butter and sauté in a frying pan. A fillet of beef is best when cooked medium rare, but should you like it well cooked give it a few more minutes of cooking. Have ready rounds of freshly made buttered toast (same size as fillets) arranged on a platter and place each cooked fillet on a round of toast. Brush the fillets with glaze viands (beef extract) and surround with horseradish sauce. Sprinkle each fillet with very finely chopped parsley, taking care not to get any in the sauce. Place a quarter of fried banana on each fillet and serve.

HORSERADISH SAUCE.

Fry in butter without browning one quarter cup of finely chopped onion, using about two tablespoons of butter. Add one cup of light cream and bring to boiling point. Strain into another sauce pan and add two egg yolks which have been beaten with two tablespoons of cream. Then add freshly grated horseradish until the sauce is quite thick. If horseradish root is not available, bottled horseradish may be used, but it must be squeezed dry of all vinegar. Season with salt. Do not allow to boil again, but the sauce can be kept at the proper temperature by placing the pan in hot water.

FRIED BANANAS.

Allow one-quarter banana for each fillet mignon a la Stanley. Peel large firm bananas and split in halves lengthwise; then cut each half across. Roll the pieces in flour and sauté in butter or deep hot fat until a golden brown. Drain on unglazed paper.

There have been several requests for Butter Cream Icing. This type of icing is especially nice on a spice cake, so I will include that recipe, too.

CINNAMON LAYER CAKE, BUTTER CREAM ICING.

One-half cup butter; 1 cup sugar; 2 eggs; ½ cup milk; ¾ cups flour; 2 ½ teaspoons baking powder; 1 tablespoon cinnamon.

Cream butter; gradually add sugar and beaten eggs. Mix and sift dry ingredients and add to first mixture, alternately with milk. Pour into two buttered layer cake pans and bake in a moderate oven 20 to 25 minutes. When layers are cool spread with butter cream icing.

BUTTER CREAM ICING. (STANDARD RECIPE).

One-quarter cup butter; 2 cups powdered sugar; ½ teaspoon vanilla; light cream (about 2 teaspoons).

Put butter in a bowl and hold at room temperature for several hours before creaming. Cream butter until very soft and gradually add the sugar, blending each addition of sugar thoroughly. As the mixture gets stiff add a few drops of light cream and a drop or two of the extract. It may be that you will use one teaspoon of light cream, but this depends on the moisture in the butter.

VARIATIONS FOR BUTTER CREAM ICING.

To vary the above formula use the yolk of an egg instead of the cream. This provides liquid and at the same time a deeper color to the icing. Now for the chocolate or mocha flavor in a butter cream icing all that is required is this: For a chocolate mocha flavor add and sift two tablespoons of cocoa to the sugar of the standard recipe and use strong coffee for liquid instead) of cream. For chocolate butter cream icing add square of chocolate (one ounce) melted to standard recipe.

November 18, 1938

Instead of serving formal dinners in the home I find ever so many ladies entertaining via the buffet table. I think it's a swell idea for two reasons—first, economy, and, second, it is not necessary to restrict the number of guests to the seating capacity of the dining-room table.

Recently I attended a very well-planned buffet supper in a small apartment, where normally only 12 at the most could be seated at the table, but at this party there were about 40 guests present.

Everything went smoothly. The aperitifs were served in the large living room, and when the dining-room doors were opened I beheld a most gorgeous display of food. There must have been 20 or more different dishes to select from. Hot foods as well as cold. Then on a side table were a dozen or more different relishes.

ALL CARVED AND READY FOR SERVICE.

I should like to enumerate some of the more important foods that appeared on the table. There was a large baked ham, half of which was neatly carved. At the opposite end of the table was a good-sized roasted turkey with a stuffing, also carved and ready for service. Several large platters contained sliced sausages of the Italian type. I counted several salads included among them stuffed tomatoes and stuffed eggs. Home-baked beans were served from a large bean pot and these made a big hit. Right alongside of the beans was a chafing dish containing piping hot miniature pork sausages. Another large chafing dish was filled with spaghetti. There was another hot food that was very popular—it was baked corned beef hash served right from the casserole. But I really think the piece de resistance was the small meat balls served with Creole sauce.

For dessert there were two large layer cakes and an assortment of small pastries. Oh, yes, I forgot to mention the several cheeses that were served from a cheese board, and they consisted of Roquefort, Swiss, Camembert, and that popular Italian cheese, Bel Paese.

RECIPES FOR TWO OF THE DISHES.

These many foods will give you an idea what to serve at a buffet supper. Space will not permit me to give you recipes for all the above-mentioned foods, but what I have in mind is to sell you on the idea of this form of eating entertainment.

MEAT BALLS, CREOLE SAUCE.

One pound chopped round steak; 1 cup bread crumbs; 2 tablespoons onions, finely minced; 2 tablespoons parsley, finely minced; 1 teaspoon salt; ⅛ teaspoon cayenne pepper; 1 egg, well beaten.

Put all ingredients together and mix thoroughly. Form into small balls about an inch and one-half in diameter. Dust lightly with flour and cook in frying pan until evenly browned. Use rendered beef suet for this purpose and use only enough to coat or grease the pan while the meat balls are browning. Then remove frying pan to oven and dot each meat ball with a bit of butter. Pour over hot creole sauce and let stand in hot oven for 10 or 15 minutes. Serve.

CREOLE SAUCE.

Two cups canned tomatoes; 1 medium-sized onion, thinly sliced; 1 green pepper, diced; ½ cup mushrooms, thinly sliced; 1 cup tomato soup (condensed); 2 tablespoons minced cooked ham; 1 teaspoon Worcestershire sauce; salt; pepper; 1 tablespoon butter.

Cover onion and green pepper with water and cook until tender, or about ten minutes. Meanwhile, sauté the sliced fresh mushrooms in butter until soft. Then add the onions, green pepper, and mushrooms to canned tomatoes and cook together for ten minutes. Stir in thick tomato soup, add minced ham, Worcestershire, and salt and pepper to taste. Just as the sauce is removed from fire add the butter and stir until blended.

Here is the glorified version of corned beef hash that was served at the buffet. I am sure that it will become one of your favorites, too. The recipe serves six:

BAKED CORNED BEEF HASH.

Four cups ground corned beef; 4 cups cold boiled potato; 1 cup onion; 1 cup water; salt and pepper; 2 tablespoons butter; 1 bottle chili sauce.

Put corned beef, potato, and onion through food chopper. Mix thoroughly and moisten with cold water. Season to taste with salt and pepper. Pack in a well-greased casserole or pan about two inches high. Dot top with bits of butter and pour chili sauce over all. Bake in moderate oven about 30 minutes.

MUSHROOMS DELICIOUS WITH MEATS.

Now that mushrooms are plentiful we could have this treat once in a while. Quite delicious when served with roast meat or broiled steak. Good also on the buffet table, but increase recipe to suit your needs.

MUSHROOM BOUCHEES.

Select the extra-large mushroom for this recipe. Wipe the cap with a damp cloth and remove the entire stem from eight large mushrooms. Chop the stems finely and cook them in two tablespoons of butter, add one tablespoon of finely chopped onion, two tablespoons of bread crumbs, three tablespoons of finely chopped cooked chicken and one teaspoon of finely chopped parsley. Moisten with meat or chicken stock and fill the mushroom caps with the mixture. Cover top with fine bread crumbs mixed with an equal quantity of grated Swiss cheese. Dot mushrooms with a small piece of butter and place on a greased baking pan. Cook in moderate over 15 or 20 minutes.

When you fancy something a little different for the vegetable course, try this:

CANNED CORN SOUFFLE.

Make a cream sauce by melting two tablespoons of butter, blending in two tablespoons of flour and gradually adding one cup of rich milk. Bring to the boiling point, stirring constantly until smooth. Remove from fire and stir in one can of corn. Season with salt and white pepper and add one-quarter cup of minced pimiento. Stir in two egg yolks which have been slightly beaten; then fold in two egg whites stiffly beaten. Pour into a buttered oven casserole dish (glass or earthen) and bake in a moderate oven for 30 minutes. Serve immediately.

November 25, 1938

When I was a young chap just out of college my father had no easy time in selling me on the idea of going into the restaurant business, especially when I was told to start in the kitchen, where my first assignment was cleaning chickens and fish.

Many a time I wanted to throw up the job, but my better judgment kept me from doing that, there was too much cookery talent all around me not to take advantage of it. I don't want to throw too many bouquets to the chef and cooks in Rector's but I say now and always will that these cooks knew their business. Mistakes were very few.

Just because I have put in this boost for Rector's please do not think for one minute that other very good restaurants did not exist. Successful restaurateurs in the days I am talking about were doing business in cities all over the country, and in every case I know of these men learned their business from the bottom up.

SOMETHING LACKING IN MODERN COOKING.

There was Boldt in Philadelphia, Kinsley in Chicago, Rector, Delmonico and Sherry in New York and many others. These gentlemen were proud of the food they served and didn't hesitate to let it be known that cookery was one of the fine arts, and I am more convinced than ever that it is.

Only today a friend of mine asked me an oft-repeated question, "Is the cooking of today as good it was in years gone by?" He had in mind, of course, restaurant cooking. I had to answer that I didn't think so. There are exceptions, but generally speaking that certain flavor, tang, or whatever you want to call it is missing.

Take, for example, that very famous restaurant, Marguery's, in Paris, France. Tourists from all over the world went to Marguery's for its specialty, fillet of sole. It was the sauce that really made the dish so delicious and when that fine old gentleman, M. Marguery, passed on, the place slowly lost its popularity and finally closed its doors.

Imported sole is almost impossible to get, but flounder when available is a good substitute. Almost any fillets of small fish could be used. Frozen fillets are in the fish markets pretty much all over the country, so use them if you are unable to get the whole fish. The object of purchasing the whole fish is to have the head, bones and akin to make the fish stock which is the base of the sauce.

RECIPES FOR FAMOUS DISH AND SAUCE.

I am going to give you the recipe for this famous dish and some time when you are in the mood to test your culinary skill try it. The white wine that is used in the sauce is not a sweet wine. Perhaps I could better compare it as a Rhine wine type, such as is made in California.

FILLET OF SOLE, MARGUERY.

Have the fish butcher remove the fillets from two flounders. Place bones, skin and heads in a stew pan. Add one pound of inexpensive fish such as flounder, halibut or cod, having it cleaned and cut in small pieces, also add ½ cup sliced carrots and one leek cut in small pieces, 2 sprigs of parsley, 10 whole peppercorns, 14 bay leaf and 2 quarts of cold water. Bring to boiling point, and simmer until fish stock is reduced to one pint, then strain. Pour a little of this fish stock (about half) over the fillets which have been seasoned with salt and a few grains of cayenne pepper and arranged in a buttered baking pan. Cover fillets with buttered paper and place in a moderate oven to poach for 15 to 20 minutes. Carefully lift the fillets out of the pan and arrange them on a hot oven proof platter. Garnish with one teaspoon of finely minced parsley, twelve small poached oysters and twelve small boiled shrimp which have been shelled and cleaned.

Now make the sauce. Pour remaining fish stock into the baking pan in which fillets were poached to recover essence in pan and simmer until quantity is reduced to three tablespoons, no more, then strain this small quantity into top part of double boiler and add four tablespoons of dry white wine, also ¼ pound of butter. Cook over hot water, stirring until butter is melted. (Have very little water in lower part of double boiler, just enough to create a gentle steam.) Then add four well beaten egg yolks, stirring constantly until sauce thickens, or about the consistency of medium cream sauce. Then pour this sauce over the fillets, oysters and shrimp and place in hot oven until glazed or lightly browned.

It was my good fortune to have worked alongside of M. Le Veau, chef at Marguery's, who made this sauce several times a day.

Lattice potatoes fried in deep hot fat would be excellent to serve with this fish.

POTATOES GAUFRETTE.

Wash and pare potatoes. Slice in lattice form, using slicer which is made for this purpose. Let stand in cold water for 30 minutes; drain and dry between towel. Fry in deep, hot fat (370°) or hot enough to brown an inch cube of bread in 60 seconds. Drain on unglazed paper and sprinkle with salt.

CUCUMBER SALAD.

Pare two medium-sized cucumbers; discard pulpy ends. Cut in very thin slices and let stand in cold water for 30 minutes. Drain on dry towel or napkin and squeeze until all water is extracted. Mix with sour cream dressing and serve on a bed of crisp lettuce leaves.

Sour Cream Dressing.

One-half pint thick sour cream, ¼ cup vinegar, 1 teaspoon salt, few grains cayenne pepper, 2 teaspoons chives, finely cut. Bunch chives together and cut finely, using sharp scissors. Dissolve salt and cayenne in vinegar. Mix all ingredients and serve.

BAKED PRUNE WHIP.

Press cooked prunes through a coarse sieve until there are two cupfuls; discard prune pits. To the prune pulp add one-half cup of sugar and cook for five minutes. Let cool and add one tablespoon of lemon juice; then fold in five egg whites which have been stiffly beaten. Have ready a buttered and sugared baking dish and pile prune whip in it. Set dish in a pan of hot water and bake about 45 minutes in a slow oven (325 degrees). May be served hot or cold with whipped cream or soft-boiled custard.

December 2, 1938

Several times in this column I have talked about what might be called the national dish of America. We know the national bird is the eagle, but there's another bird, the turkey, that could easily be regarded as one of the national foods.

A fine, big, freshly killed turkey, properly roasted with all the trimmings, is about the most festive food that can be placed on the dining table. I hope it won't be far off when we may find in the markets fresh killed turkeys the year around. I have heard that attempts are being made in several states to bring this about, However, we do not know that the season for fresh turkeys is considerably longer and the price much lower than a few years ago. There is also an effort being made to produce a small bird, suitable for a family of two, three, or four. Such a bird could be split and broiled.

SERVED IN OTHER WAYS AFTER FIRST MEAL.

A roast turkey of medium weight, let's say 12 pounds, has more possibilities than any food I know of. After the bird has made its first appearance it is natural to serve it cold. Or it could be sliced, heated in its own gravy and served on toast or in a border of rice. You could, on the following day, if the bird holds out, serve it a la king or in the form of turkey hash. After all the meat has been removed from the bones there's still one more dish that can be prepared and that is turkey soup.

In preparing a turkey for roasting, much care should be given to the stuffing. Many people like a wet stuffing and many others prefer a dry stuffing. We should be able to please all by having both kinds. The breast stuffing could be dry and the frame stuffing wet, or vice versa.

If the family is fond of stuffing it would be a good idea to make an extra quantity to cook on the side. This is easily accomplished by putting the extra stuffing in a well-buttered baking dish about one hour before the turkey is cooked, basting at fifteen-minute intervals with drippings from the roasting pan.

SUGGESTIONS FOR ENJOYABLE TURKEY DINNER.

It is no longer the traditional Thanksgiving turkey, but rather a popular bird to serve all through the holiday season. Any suggestions found in the recipes which follow, I trust, will make your turkey dinner a most enjoyable one.

ROAST TURKEY.

Have butcher prepare turkey for roasting, taking care to make incisions as small as possible. Remove pin feathers, singe hairs and wash. Pat dry with clean towel or napkin. Fill breast and frame with stuffing, sew skin together and truss, using white string for the purpose. The wings are folded under in such a way that they will hold close to the frame (the butcher will show you how to do this) and the legs are tied tightly to the tail of the bird.

Sprinkle turkey with salt and rub entire surface with soft butter. Place turkey in large baking pan, lay two thin slices of salt pork over breast and start to cook in hot oven (450 degrees) for 10 minutes. Reduce heat to moderate (325 degrees) and baste every 15 minutes until turkey is cooked, allowing about three and one-half to four hours for a medium-sized turkey of 10 to 12 pounds.

Do not put water in the pan with the turkey, but start basting of turkey after first 15 minutes' cooking with one-half cup butter melted in one-half cup of hot water. When this has been used up, baste from baking pan. If breast of turkey browns too fast cover it with a piece of white buttered paper. Remove turkey to large, hot platter and make gravy.

GIBLET GRAVY.

Cover gizzard, heart and neck with boiling water, add a stalk of celery, one onion, two sprigs of parsley and one-half teaspoon of salt. Let simmer until giblets are tender or about one and one-half hours, then add the liver and cook rapidly for ten minutes. Put gizzard, heart and liver in chopping bowl and chop finely. Pour off all but four tablespoons of drippings remaining in roasting pan, blend in three tablespoons of flour and gradually add two cups of the strained giblet stock, stirring constantly until boiling point is reached. Season to taste and strain into sauceboat; add chopped giblets and serve.

SAVORY BREAD STUFFING.
(For Turkey.)

Three-fourth cup butter, ½ cup chopped onions, 12 cups stale bread crumbs, 1 teaspoon salt, ½ teaspoon pepper, ¼ cup parsley, finely chopped, ¼ cup celery leaves, finely chopped, 1 tablespoon poultry seasoning, ½ cup hot water.

Put one-half of butter in heavy frying pan; add onions and cook over low heat until soft, taking care that butter and onions retain original color. Meanwhile put bread crumbs in large mixing bowl, add salt, pepper, poultry seasoning, parsley and celery leaves and toss all together lightly. Then add partially cooked onions and moisten with balance of butter melted in hot water. Mix thoroughly and stuff bird.

SAUSAGE STUFFING.
(For Turkey Craw.)

One-half pound sausage meat, 3 cups stale bread crumbs, 1 tablespoon sausage drippings, 1 tablespoon parsley, finely chopped, 1 teaspoon salt, ⅛ teaspoon pepper, 1 teaspoon poultry seasoning, 2 tablespoons melted butter.

Cook sausage meat over moderate flame; drain off all but one tablespoon of sausage fat. Remove from fire, add bread crumbs, parsley and seasonings. Toss together lightly and moisten with melted butter. Fill crop of turkey with mixture, packing it in lightly.

CHESTNUT AND RAISIN STUFFING.
(For Turkey.)

Three pounds French chestnuts, 6 cups stale bread crumbs, 1 cup large seedless raisins, ¼ cup onion, finely chopped; ½ cup butter, 1 tablespoon sugar, grated rind of 1 lemon, 1 teaspoon salt, hot milk to moisten.

Cover chestnuts with boiling water and simmer until soft, about 35 minutes. Drain, and while still warm remove shells and skin. Put half of them through the ricer and break or chop balance into small pieces. Cover raisins with boiling water and let stand for one hour; drain. Add sugar and grated rind of raisins. Cook onion colorless in butter for about five minutes. Combine prepared ingredients, add salt, tossing lightly and using only enough hot milk to moisten.

Next week I am going to give you a complete Christmas menu with as many recipes as space will allow.

REQUESTED RECIPE.
Thousand Island Dressing.

One cup mayonnaise, ⅓ cup chili sauce, 1 tablespoon green pepper, finely chopped, 4 stuffed olives, finely chopped, 1 teaspoon onion or chives, finely chopped. Stir chili sauce into mayonnaise, add finely chopped ingredients and mix. Just before serving fold in one-half cup of whipped cream.

December 9, 1938

Last week I promised to give you a complete Christmas menu, so here we go. Serving of aperitifs is popular in many homes and that calls for appetizers, or call them hors d'oeuvres if you want to be a little ritzy.

For the first course at the table I would suggest serving crabmeat ravigote, and before we go any further let me say a word about crabmeat. The fresh meat that is taken out of the crabs from the waters of Chesapeake Bay is extremely perishable and cannot be shipped too far inland. This need not disconcert you, because the regular canned crabmeat available in most stores will serve the purpose just as well.

Of course, you will have on the table the usual relishes, such as ripe and green olives, salted nuts and celery hearts cut in lengthwise quarters. I think a soup should follow, and since fresh mushrooms are plentiful and reasonable it would be a treat to serve cream of fresh mushroom soup.

Now let us get down to the main course, which will be a roast turkey with all the trimmings. If you decide not to have a chestnut stuffing. then by all means serve puree of chestnuts as an accompaniment or vegetable. We must have sweet potatoes with our turkey and let them be candied sweets or mashed sweets with a marshmallow topping. Cranberries, of course, and it's a good idea to serve them both ways—as a jelly and as a sauce. We will want a green vegetable and this could be either peas or string beans cut in lengthwise pieces, which is the most attractive way to serve them.

Now comes the salad. This should be rather simple, I think, because of the number of courses served. Any salad greens such as romaine, escarole, chicory, lettuce or endive, served crisp and cold with a light fresh dressing, would be perfect. An added touch could be a slice or two of avocado pear served on top of the individual salads.

For dessert no Christmas dinner is complete without plum pudding or mince pie, although ice cream is gaining ground, especially in families where there are children. A novel way to serve cheese with mince pie is to melt it as a rabbit and pour it over the pie. This is called a "slip on" and originated in our old time chop houses or taverns as they were sometimes called. It sounds terrific, doesn't it? But, anyway, it has an advantage, and that is serving of cheese as a separate course.

CRABMEAT RAVIGOTE, À LA RECTOR.

One pound crabmeat, ¼ cup vinegar, salt and pepper to taste, 2 tablespoons pimiento finely chopped, 2 tablespoons chives finely chopped, 2 tablespoons vinegar pickles finely chopped, ½ cup mayonnaise, pimiento strips.

Canned or fresh crabmeat may be used. Pour vinegar over crabmeat and let marinate 15 minutes. Squeeze vinegar from crabmeat and season with salt and pepper. Add finely chopped pimiento, chives, and pickle. Then add mayonnaise and toss lightly until thoroughly mixed. Serve on crisp lettuce leaf. Decorate with a light sprinkle of paprika and pimiento strips crossed on top.

CREAM OF MUSHROOM SOUP.

One-half pound mushrooms, 6 cups white stock, 5 tablespoons butter, 5 tablespoons flour, ½ cup cream, lemon rind.

Wash mushrooms. Chop or slice them into small pieces. Cook mushrooms 20 minutes with white stock. Strain stock into another saucepan and force mushrooms through a sieve into stock. Reheat, thicken with butter and flour creamed together. Bring to boiling point, stirring until smooth, then add cream and season to taste with salt and pepper. Rub the soup plates or cups with lemon rind, as this imparts a delightful flavor.

CHESTNUT PUREE.

Here is the recipe for chestnut puree to be served as a vegetable:

Two pounds French or Italian chestnuts, ½ teaspoon salt, ¼ teaspoon celery salt, ⅛ teaspoon white pepper, hot milk.

Cover chestnuts with boiling water and cook until tender or about 30 minutes. Drain; when cool enough to handle, remove shells and brown skin. Mash chestnuts by either pressing them through a ricer or by mashing several at a time with the prongs of a strong fork. The idea is to work fast, as shelling and mashing should be done while chestnuts are warm. Add seasonings; beat in a little hot milk at a time until mixture becomes light heat over low flame and serve.

CANDIED SWEET POTATOES.

Select small sweet potatoes for this purpose and of uniform size. Cover potatoes with boiling water and parboil for 15 minutes. Drain, peel and cut potatoes in halves lengthwise. Arrange potatoes in a buttered baking dish, sprinkling each layer with brown sugar and dotting liberally with bits of butter. Bake in moderate oven (325 degrees) for one hour. For the average family cook six or eight potatoes and use about one-half cup of butter and a scant cup of brown sugar.

MARSHMALLOW SWEET POTATOES.

Cover sweet potatoes with boiling water and cook until soft. Peel and mash. To every four cups of mashed potatoes add a scant teaspoon of salt and three tablespoons of butter; whisk all together and place in well-buttered baking dish. Cover entire top with marshmallows and set in moderate oven until marshmallows melt, then brown quickly under low broiler flame.

SPICED CRANBERRIES.

One pound cranberries; 2 cups sugar; 1 cup water; ½ cup vinegar; 12 whole cloves; stick cinnamon (3-inch); grated rind of 1 orange.

Bring sugar, water and vinegar to boiling point. Add cloves and stick cinnamon tied in small cheese cloth bag. Then add cranberries and cook until skins break open. Remove spice bag, add grated rind of orange, pour into sterilized jars and seal.

CRANBERRY JELLY.

Wash and pick over one pound of cranberries. Place in a saucepan and add just enough water to cover. Cook twenty minutes. Strain through a sieve, pressing as much of the pulp through as possible. For each cup of juice add one-half cup of sugar and cook rapidly for five minutes. Pour into fancy molds or jelly glasses. If wanted for future use have glasses sterilized and cover with paraffin.

December 16, 1938

Long before the super food stores made their appearance, practically every city of any size or consequence had its own public food markets.

I well remember one of those public markets—it was in Baltimore, and I guess it's still there. Well, I would spend a whole morning or an afternoon around the food stalls and enjoy it quite as much as the diversion of a good show or the thrill of listening to a fine symphony orchestra.

Fresh produce or fine cuts of meat displayed with taste is a commanding sight and one which never fails to attract my attention. It was the custom in former days for a restauranteur to go to market and make the necessary purchases for the day. I did it myself many times, alternating the task with my father. Going to market in the wee small hours of the morning, after the close of business, might seem like hard work, and I suppose it was, but we enjoyed it, regardless of some loss of sleep.

Take, for example, the matter of selecting cheese, I mean the cheese that we used for making Welsh rabbits (it's spelled rabbit, not rarebit). Perhaps a whole day or a good part of it would be spent testing and tasting these cheeses in order to get the one that had that certain tang or flavor that would produce an excellent Welsh rabbit. Fifty of these cheeses wore purchased at a time to be held for us: and please remember that the success of a rabbit is in the quality of the cheese. A fine rich medium sharp and aged American cheese is the kind to purchase.

WHY VEAL IS A EUROPEAN DELICACY.

While we are on the subject of public markets I would like to relate briefly of one I visited in Florence, Italy, where I purchased veal—young, tender, milk-fed veal, carved by the butcher right there before me. This veal was as white as chicken meat and could easily have been passed off as such. That very evening I had it for dinner cooked au Marsala and it was so deliciously tender that I could well understand why veal is so largely consumed throughout Central Europe.

Veal is considered a delicacy in Europe and the reason that this is so is because the calves are slaughtered at a very young age. We do not slaughter our calves quite so young, but we do have fancy veal which is obtainable but scarce and rather expensive.

ESCALLOPINE OF VEAL AU MARSALA.

Veal callops (1½ pounds), ½ cup grated Parmesan cheese, ¼ cup clarified butter, 1 cup thinly sliced mushrooms, 2 tablespoons butter, salt, light pinch cayenne, 1 teaspoon extract of beef, 2 tablespoons hot water, 4 tablespoons Marsala or sherry.

Callops of veal may be cut from the loin or fillet, but they are more often cut from the cutlet or leg. Have the butcher cut them in slices about three-eighths of an inch thick and about two inches in diameter. Dip callops in grated Parmesan cheese and sauté in clarified butter until lightly browned. In a separate pan cook thinly sliced mushrooms, using about two tablespoons butter; season mushrooms with salt and cayenne. When callops are cooked arrange them on a hot platter, having them overlap each other. Add extract of beef dissolved in hot water to essence in pan along with a tablespoon of fresh butter. Stir over very low heat until mixed and essence is dissolved. Add Marsala or sherry wine; shake pan and give one minute of high heat, pour sauce over escallopes, garnish with mushrooms and serve at once. Fresh green peas make an excellent accompaniment.

CLARIFIED BUTTER.

Melt butter in saucepan over low heat. Skim top of froth, remove from heat and let settle. Carefully pour melted butter into dish, leaving salt on the bottom to be discarded.

FAMILY RECIPE FOR A RICH VEAL DISH.

Here is a dandy family recipe that I want you to have. While, it resembles a stew or fricassee, it is much richer than either of these, as it is finished off with egg yolks and cream. Sounds good, doesn't it?

BLANQUETTE OF VEAL.

Two pounds breast veal, 1 medium-sized onion, 1 clove, 1 carrot, 1 leek, 2 sprigs of parsley, small bay leaf, bit of thyme, roux, 2 egg yolks, 3 tablespoons heavy cream.

Have veal cut in uniform-sized pieces that will yield about six to the pound. Put in stewpan, cover with cold water, add onion stuck with clove, carrot, leek, parsley, bay leaf and thyme. Bring to boiling point and skim. Cover pan and let simmer about one and one-half hours or until meat is tender. Season with one-half teaspoon of salt 20 minutes before meat is cooked. Transfer the pieces of veal to a hot dish, strain stock, discarding the vegetables. Thicken stock (there should be about four cups) with roux, bring to boiling point and let boil for two minutes. Add egg yolks and cream beaten together. Heat but do not allow to boil. Strain sauce over meat and serve in a border of mashed potatoes that have been whipped very light.

Small white onions boiled in salted water until soft, then drained and seasoned with white pepper and just enough butter to moisten, would round out a complete meal.

Make roux as follows: Melt 3 tablespoons of butter over low heat and gradually stir in 4 tablespoons of flour. When thoroughly blended (do not allow to discolor) it is ready to be used as thickening agent.

APPLE SNOW.

Steam quartered apples until soft enough to press through a sieve. For every cup of apple pulp allow the whites of 3 eggs beaten until stiff with ½ cup of sugar and flavored with 1 tablespoon of lemon juice. Fold apple pulp into meringue and pile lightly in large glass dish. Chill and serve with boiled custard sauce.

BOILED CUSTARD SAUCE
(Liquid or Soft Custard).

Two eggs or 4 egg yolks, ½ cup sugar, 1 teaspoon cornstarch, pinch of salt, 1 pint scalded milk, 1 teaspoon vanilla.

Scald milk in top part of double boiler. Beat slightly; gradually add sugar, cornstarch and salt sifted together. Pour hot milk over egg mixture, stirring until sugar is dissolved. Cook over hot water, stirring constantly until custard thickens and coats the spoon. Remove from heat, strain at once and stir until slightly cooled. Add flavoring, chill and serve.

December 22, 1938

Before I say another word let me wish you and yours a Merry Christmas. Today I am drinking a toast to you all. It's to "your health and happiness—may you live long and prosper."

If some old-timers happen to read that toast they will no doubt be reminded of that fine actor, the late Joseph Jefferson, who repeatedly offered it in that great stage success of his, "Rip Van Winkle."

Nothing in my life has made me so genuinely happy as the letters I have received from readers of this column. Operating a successful restaurant for many years was fun—aside from the profits. It was the glamour of it all that made it so interesting, I guess. So a long ways back I had hoped that some day I might share with you all of the knowledge that I have gained in the art of cookery.

OURS THE FINEST FOODS IN THE WORLD.
A restaurant noted for good food and service has its following, of course, and naturally it becomes a financial success. It's nice to be in a cash business and have the customers thank you on the way out, praising the food and service of a fine meal.

What is there in the home that causes more happiness or real contentment than well prepared food? I don't mean that we have to have the cookery knowledge of famous foreign chefs to be able to prepare delicious meals. We have in this great country of ours the finest foods in the world, and you know when you get right down to the basic needs in a kitchen you can do wonders with butter, cream and eggs. These are the culinary artist's pigments and without them we wouldn't have any kitchen.

Wild ducks were featured on the Rector menu. Canvasbacks and redheads were the most popular and the most expensive. We were about the first to introduce corn-fed mallards, which were held in captivity and fed corn for a certain period of time until they were purged of the fishy flavor that is so characteristic of the mallard duck.

WILD DUCK ROASTED AND RARE.

There is only one way to cook a wild duck and that is to roast it. No stuffing is required. After the duck is plucked and drawn, the liver is set aside to be added to the sauce later on. The duck is trussed and seasoned with salt and pepper and a thin slice of salt pork is spread over the breast. A very hot oven is required (500 degrees) and the duck is cooked in 18 to 20 minutes.

Most every gourmet who ordered wild duck in Rector's insisted that it should not be overcooked. They all wanted it rare and one of our customers was so particular about having it rare that he explained to me just how he cooked wild duck in his own home. He would say to the duck, "Duck meet oven and oven meet duck." That was his idea of how rare it should be cooked.

After the duck was roasted it was brought to the patron on a large silver platter. Then the two whole breasts were neatly carved from the bird, not sliced. The legs were removed and the meat carved from them. This procedure was the start for the delicious sauce that is always served with wild duck. The whole breasts are left on the silver platter and the carcass and legs are put in the duck press. The wheel of the press is then turned until the bones are crushed and every drop of juice is extracted. The juice runs off in a small sauce boat.

JUICE ADDED UNDER SLOW HEAT.

Now the silver platter with the whole breasts of duck is set over a chafing dish frame with the alcohol burner directly under the platter. The extracted juice is poured over the breasts and seasoned with a little salt and cayenne pepper. To this heated juice one teaspoon of extract of beef is added and also one tablespoon of currant jelly. This sauce is spooned over the breasts a number of times and when these two ingredients are blended add a few drops of Worcestershire and two or three tablespoons of Madeira or sherry.

Let all this heat together without actual boiling, spooning the sauce over the breasts until they are well saturated. The breasts are then placed on the dinner plate. The raw duck liver, which has been pressed through a fine sieve, is then added to the sauce in the platter stirred and thoroughly heated (not boiled) and immediately poured over the breasts and served. You now have wild duck a la presse.

HOMINY AND A SALAD COMPLETE THE PICTURE.

Fried hominy is always served with wild duck and usually grilled sweet potatoes. A simple salad of chopped celery thoroughly mixed with a French dressing and served on a light bed of lettuce just about completes the picture.

The fine hominy is used in this recipe. Put one cup of fine hominy in top part of double boiler and mix it with one cup of cold water. Then pour three cups of boiling water over it, adding one teaspoon of salt. Stir over direct heat for five minutes; put top part of boiler over lower part and cook over hot water for one hour. Pack in greased breadpan and let stand for several hours or overnight until solid. Cut in slices one-half inch thick and trim slices into perfect diamond shape of four inches long and three inches wide. Fry in deep hot fat until browned. Drain on unglazed paper and serve.

SAUCE FOR DUCK SERVED AT TABLE.

If you haven't a duck press but are fortunate enough to get wild duck, then I would suggest that you follow directions for roasting the duck, giving it five or ten minutes longer in the oven. Serve the whole duck on the platter to be carved at the table with this fine sauce.

Cumberland Sauce.

Three tablespoons red currant jelly, 2 tablespoons port wine, 2 tablespoons orange juice, 1 tablespoon lemon juice, 1 teaspoon mixed mustard, 1 teaspoon paprika, ½ teaspoon ground ginger, 3 tablespoons orange rind, finely shredded.

Melt jelly over low fire until liquid. Cool, add port wine, orange juice, lemon juice and spices. Cover orange rind with cold water, bring to a boil and drain. Add blanched orange rind to first mixture and serve.

Now a perfectly easy way to prepare wild duck, especially if you have an abundance of them, is to take a sharp knife and follow the breast bone, cutting through the feathers and skin. Carefully cut the skin away from the entire breast. Now take the knife and follow the breast cutting it away from the frame. The breasts are then sautéed in butter, about seven minutes to each side. It may sound extravagant to discard the carcass of the duck, but after all the breast is about all there is to eat on a wild duck and this method saves time, as the duck is not plucked or cleaned.

December 30, 1938

May I take this opportunity of wishing you all a happy, happy, happetizing new year, and also may the new year be chock full of prosperity along with an abundance of good health. Do you know that the custom of welcoming in the new year that is so popular in restaurants nowadays is comparatively new? Well, I'll tell you just about when it started. During the early nineties in New York and Chicago small groups of people thought it would be a good idea to step out that night, first attending the theater and then a late supper in their favorite restaurant so that they could, at midnight, drink a toast to their friends and to all the good things that the new year would bring.

Each year the occasion gained momentum and really became an established custom about the turn of the century. Just to give you an idea what a golden harvest New Year's Eve is for the restaurant man, here are the figures: Our seating capacity in Rector's normally was about 1,300, but by adding more tables and chairs thereby seating more people, increased the number to 1,500.

BIG DAY'S BUSINESS FOR ONE NIGHT.
For a ten-dollar note we served a full-course supper—it was more like a banquet. Invitations were sent out to our customers, and the response for tables was always terrific.

Besides, each reservation was accompanied with a check, which meant that there was $15,000 received and a complete sellout a week or ten days in advance of December 31.

Now we come to the beverage sale of the evening. Mixed drinks were taboo that night—champagne and only champagne was served. The cash registers showed that $18,000 was spent in wine, making the total receipts $33,000. A handsome day's business, I would say.

When I look back and recall the many brilliant New Year's Eve affairs we had in Rector's which were interrupted with the advent of prohibition, I made a resolution there and then that that night is one night I would steer clear of restaurants.

BROILED VENISON STEAK COOKED RARE.

The other day a friend of mine presented me with some venison, consisting of two steaks and a shoulder cut. The meat was properly aged, so I proceeded to cook the steaks first, which is indeed very simple. Remember that the tender cuts of a doe or buck can be cooked exactly like any other tender cuts of meat—that is, broiling, roasting, or sautéing. The coarser or less tender cuts are put in a marinade for one to three days, at the end of which time they are ready to be pot roasted or braised in the oven.

We broiled the two venison steaks, having them cooked rare. They were spread with fresh butter and seasoned with pepper and salt when they left the broiler and currant jelly was served with them. You see, broiling a venison steak isn't any different from broiling a beef steak. Now if you should want to cook them in the frying pan, grease the pan well with a piece of beef suet so the steaks will not stick, but at no time have a surplus of melted fat or grease in the pan.

RAGOUT OF VENISON A CULINARY TREAT.

A few days passed and then I cooked the shoulder cut. Since I decided to make this into a ragout, I cut the meat into two-inch cubes. This meat I dropped into a crock along with 2 cups of red wine, a claret type, and then I placed the crock in the refrigerator for hours. From this point on follow my recipe.

If you have, say, 2 pounds of venison meat, place the meat in a large saucepan containing 4 tablespoons of hot fat. Beef fat or suet rendered into the pan is fine or salt pork can be rendered. Sauté the marinated meat over a hot fire, turning on all sides until browned. This will take about five minutes. Then add one onion finely chopped, a pinch of thyme, one bay leaf, one-half teaspoon of freshly ground black pepper, one teaspoon of salt and one tablespoon of finely chopped bacon. Now here is where you add the wine in which the meat was marinated, plus a cup of good beef stock. Cover the saucepan and let cook slowly for about one hour, then add one dozen very small onions and continue cooking for another hour.

In the meantime sauté 12 or 15 medium-sized mushrooms in butter, turning them frequently until they are cooked and nicely browned. Serve ragout on a large hot platter garnished with the sauteed mushrooms. Sprinkle a tablespoon of finely chopped parsley over all. And there you have, my friends, a culinary treat that will long be remembered.

UNUSUAL AND SIMPLE CAKE RECIPE.

In testing a batch of new recipes I think you should have this one in your collection. It is somewhat unusual and extremely simple to follow:

Honey Chocolate Cake.

Two and one-half cups cake flour, 1 teaspoon baking powder, ¾ teaspoon soda, 1 teaspoon vanilla, ¾ cup honey,

¾ cup brown sugar, ½ cup shortening, ½ cup cocoa, 2 eggs, 1¼ cups sour milk, ½ teaspoon salt.

Thoroughly cream honey, sugar and shortening. Add cocoa and stir well. Add eggs one at a time and stir vigorously. Add sour milk and sifted dry ingredients and stir lightly. Add vanilla. Pour in well-greased layer tins and bake in moderate oven (375°) for 40 minutes. Makes three nine-inch layers. Put the layers together with apricot marmalade or peach jam and cover cake with chocolate icing.

Chocolate Icing.

One and three-quarter cups sugar, ¾ cups hot water, 4 squares chocolate, ½ teaspoon vanilla.

Boil sugar and water together until it thickens and spins a thread when dropped from spoon. Melt chocolate over hot water. Gradually pour sirup on melted chocolate, beating until icing is of right consistency to spread, then add vanilla and spread icing on cake at once.

INDIVIDUAL SPONGE BASKETS.

You may use your own recipe for sponge cake, but I would like you to have this recipe of mine containing potato flour, as the cake has a delicate texture:

Three eggs, ¾ cup sugar, ½ cup potato flour, ¼ teaspoon cream of tartar, ⅛ teaspoon salt, ½ teaspoon vanilla.

Separate eggs. Beat whites until stiff. Beat yolks until light and creamy, and gradually beat in sugar. Mix potato flour, cream of tartar, and salt together and sift into yolk and sugar mixture. Add vanilla and fold in egg whites. Bake in ungreased muffin tins in moderate oven (350 degrees) 25 minutes. When cakes are cool scoop out centers and fill with candied fruit and cream made as follows:

One cup heavy cream whipped, ¼ cup candied cherries finely chopped, ¼ cup candied pineapple finely chopped, and ¼ cup walnuts finely chopped.

Make handles for baskets by steaming long thin strips of angelica in top part of double boiler until somewhat soft and flexible.

January 6, 1939

With all the holiday feasting over, a change in diet should be welcome about this time. Fish or shellfish offer a delightful change whereby simple, but satisfying meals can be prepared.

At this time of the year oysters are particularly good, and I wonder if you include them often enough in your menu planning. In looking through my files I find ever so many mouth-watering recipes on oysters (recipes which were specialties of Rector's) that I have decided you should have these in your files, too.

Oysters in the shell are not obtainable too far distant from the Atlantic Coast, but "loose" oysters which are known as bulk oysters are shipped to sections pretty far inland. You can purchase them by measure or count. These bulk oysters are opened right at the source of supply, properly chilled, and little or no time is lost in shipping them to the markets. Of course, oysters are perishable, but proper refrigeration during transit ensures real freshness when brought to the consumer.

The other afternoon I stepped into a neighborhood food store and a tub of these bulk oysters caught my eye. They were an appetizing picture—medium-sized, plump, white—so I purchased two dozen and had them for dinner that night. We have a favorite way in our household of preparing oysters in this simple fashion that I will tell you about first. They are cooked sauté in a heavy frying pan, or if you would like to use the chafing dish and do them right at the table, as we frequently do, you will find it the best of fun. Here is how:

OYSTER SAUTÉ.

Select medium-sized oysters and allow six or eight to each portion. Lay them on a clean towel or napkin and pat until dry. Season with salt, pepper, and a few grains of cayenne and dip lightly in flour.

Sauté in butter until lightly browned, turning the oysters but once during the cooking. Have ready some freshly made buttered toast, cut triangle shape, and when oysters are cooked, arrange them in the center of the plate. Put two pieces of toast on each plate, having the long side of the triangle banking the oysters. Squeeze a few drops of lemon juice over the oysters and sprinkle with finely chopped parsley.

Now here is a dandy recipe calling for oysters in the shell. However, if you live in a section where oysters in the shell are not obtainable but bulk oysters are, you may purchase scallop shells from your local household store. These are nice to have for many other dishes, notably creamed fish served au gratin. They are not expensive and I know that you will enjoy having them in your kitchen equipment.

OYSTERS CASINO.

Select large oysters for this recipe and have them opened on the deep shell. Allow eight to each portion. Arrange oysters on the deep shell in a shallow baking pan which has been prepared with a layer of rock salt. Imbed the oysters firmly in the rock salt, as this will hold them steady while cooking. Season with salt, a speck of cayenne pepper, and paprika. To each oyster add a pinch of finely chopped green pepper, a pinch of finely chopped pimento, and a piece of sliced bacon cut the same size as the oyster. Broil under moderate flame until cooked. Bacon will cook first, so when both sides are broiled remove it to a warm dish while oysters and peppers cook eight or ten minutes longer. Keep oysters moist by adding a bit of butter or oyster liquor while cooking. Serve in the shells and garnish each oyster with the small piece of broiled bacon and a tiny sprig of parsley.

BASS PORTUGAISE.

A whole baked fish such as bass, bluefish, cod, or whitefish served a la Portuguese would be nice for a change.

Have the fish cleaned and prepared for baking, leaving the head on. Select one weighing three pounds or over. Rub fish with olive oil and season with salt and pepper. Place it in a butter-greased baking dish, sprinkle a tablespoon of finely chopped onion over the top, and add four tablespoons of dry white wine to the pan. Bake in a moderate oven 35 to 40 minutes, basting occasionally with the wine. Then pour two cups of Portugaise sauce over the fish, sprinkle bread crumbs over the top, dot with small bits of butter and return to oven until crumbs are browned. Serve with parsley potatoes.

SAUCE PORTUGAISE.

One green pepper, thinly sliced, 1 medium-sized onion, thinly sliced, ½ cup mushrooms, thinly sliced, 2 cups canned tomatoes, 12 olives, thinly sliced, 2 tablespoons butter, 2 tablespoons flour, salt and pepper

Cover green pepper, onion, and mushrooms with water and cook until tender or about 10 minutes. Then add canned tomatoes and thinly sliced stuffed olives (pimento stuffed olives) and bring to boiling point. Thicken sauce with butter and flour creamed together and let boil two minutes longer.

CHEESE CAKE.

Here is a recipe that I have had several requests for. It is an old-fashioned recipe but still popular!

Crust—One cup butter, 1 cup sugar, 1 egg, ⅓ cup milk, 3 cups flour, ½ teaspoon soda, 1 teaspoon flavoring extract.

Filling—One and one-half cups of cottage cheese, ½ cup sugar, 3 tablespoons cream, grated rind of 1 lemon, 3 eggs, 1 egg yolk.

Crust—Cream butter; add sugar gradually and cream well together. Add unbeaten egg and beat thoroughly. Add milk and when well mixed fold in flour which has been sifted with soda. Add flavoring. Roll out to one-quarter inch thickness and line pie or layer pan.

Filling—Mix together cottage cheese, sugar, cream, and grated lemon rind; then add well beaten eggs. Fill lined pie or layer pan and bake in a moderate oven (350 degrees) about 35 minutes.

January 13, 1939

A short time ago I read in the papers that President Roosevelt is a devotee of scrambled eggs for breakfast, and aren't we all? Since then I have been wondering just how the cook in the White House prepares the scrambled eggs, as it's a most delectable dish when done a certain way, and I will tell you what that way is now.

Once upon a time, and that was way back in 1902, I had lunch in the famous William the Conqueror Restaurant located at Mont San-Michel in Normandy, France. This restaurant was owned and managed by a woman and her name was Madame Poulard, and besides she did much of the cooking herself. The specialties, de la Maison, were eggs. Her omelets were absolutely perfect—nicely browned on the outside and moist inside.

AS SIMPLE AS IT IS GOOD.

The egg dish that made such a hit with me was the way she did scrambled eggs, and it's so simple that perhaps you too will wonder why you didn't think of it yourself. First of all madame insisted that eggs should be beaten in a wooden bowl with a wooden spoon, which is sound figuring as I will explain later.

The eggs were gently beaten and one tablespoon of Normandy cream was added for each egg along with a little salt and white pepper. Instead of cooking the eggs in skillet as most cooks do, the bain-Marie (double boiler) was brought into play. The water in the lower part was boiling and a tablespoon of butter put in the upper part to melt. The eggs were then poured in and gentle stirring started immediately and constantly until the scrambled eggs were sufficiently set to be served.

Naturally, without direct heat under the eggs, they cook slowly, but that's the trick and why they are when cooked so light, fluffy and tender. Smooth—never hard or lumpy. The theory of beating eggs in wood with wood is that it is less harsh than china or metal. We all know that beating an egg cooks it, so Poulard's method was the most gentle that could be employed to prepare them for cooking over steam in the bain-Marie.

SOMETHING DIFFERENT IN A CHICKEN RECIPE.
I am sure you will welcome a chicken recipe which is a little different. All I ask you to do is read it carefully and unless I am greatly mistaken you will not delay too long in trying it.

CHICKEN TETTRAZINI.
Select a young chicken weighing about 2½ pounds. Have it cut in four pieces. Cover with boiling water and simmer until tender, adding a little salt to the water in season. When the chicken is cooked allow to cool in the broth; then shred chicken meat into fine pieces, putting the skin and bones back into the broth. Bring to boiling point and let simmer for 45 minutes. Remove cover from saucepan and let broth boil furiously for 10 or 15 minutes, as this will reduce the broth to about two cupfuls.

Meanwhile thinly slice one-quarter pound of mushrooms and sauté them in butter over moderate heat until soft and lightly browned. Break one-half pound of Italian spaghetti into small pieces and cook in a large amount of boiling salted water until tender, or about 15 minutes.

Make a cream sauce as follows: Melt 2 tablespoons of butter, blending in 2 tablespoons of flour and gradually add the hot strained chicken broth (about 2 cupfuls), stirring until perfectly smooth and boiling point is reached. Then stir in one cup of heavy cream and three tablespoons of dry sherry wine. Divide the sauce, add the shredded chicken to one-half the cooked spaghetti and mushrooms to the remaining half. Put the spaghetti half into a baking dish, making a hole in the center and banking it around the side of the dish. Pour chicken half in the center, sprinkle grated Parmesan cheese over the top and bake in a moderate oven until lightly browned—about 10 minutes.

CORKING GOOD WAYS TO PREPARE SHRIMPS.

In looking through my index file I find that very few recipes have been given on shrimps during the past year, so I have picked out three corking good recipes for you to try.

SHRIMPS À LA CREOLE.

One pound of fresh or canned shrimps, 1 medium-sized onion, 1 green pepper, diced, ½ cup mushrooms, thinly sliced, 2 cups canned tomatoes, 1 cup tomato soup (condensed), 2 tablespoons minced cooked ham, 1 teaspoon Worcestershire sauce, salt, pepper, 1 tablespoon butter, boiled rice.

If fresh shrimps are used cook them in boiling water for 15 minutes. Drain; remove shells and black vein. Canned shrimps are all ready to be used and need no cooking. Cover onion and green pepper with water and cook until tender or about 10 minutes. In the meantime sauté the sliced mushrooms in butter until soft. Then add the onions, green pepper and mushrooms to canned tomatoes and cook together for 10 minutes. Stir in thick tomato soup, add minced ham, Worcestershire, and salt and pepper to taste. Add shrimps and bring to boiling point. Just before serving add butter and stir until blended. Serve in a ring or border of plain boiled rice.

MINCED SHRIMPS LOUISIANNE.

One pound of fresh or canned shrimps, 2 tablespoons butter, 1 tablespoon minced onion, 2 cups canned cream of tomato soup, ½ teaspoon salt, pinch of cayenne pepper, 1 teaspoon Worcestershire sauce, patty shells or toast.

Cover fresh shrimps with boiling water and cook for 15 minutes. Drain; remove shells and black vein and cut shrimps into small pieces. Canned shrimps are cooked and need only be minced. Melt butter and cook minced onion colorless for five minutes. Add cream of tomato soup and seasonings and bring to boiling point. Then add minced shrimps and heat thoroughly. Serve in patty shells or on freshly made toast.

FRIED SHRIMPS, MAR DONG.

Two cups of cooked shrimps, 1 cup of sifted bread crumbs, 2 eggs, 3 tablespoons cold water, ⅔ cup mayonnaise, ⅓ cup Bengal chutney (puree).

Remove shells from shrimps and split half through convex side removing black vein at the same time. Spread shrimps open but do not split in halves. Dip each shrimp in sifted crumbs and then in egg which has been beaten with water. Dip again in bread crumbs and fry in deep hot fat (hot enough to brown a one-inch cube of bread in 60 seconds) until nicely browned. Serve with sauce which is made by stirring the chutney puree into the mayonnaise until thoroughly mixed.

January 20, 1939

One of our readers who lives down Long Island way writes as follows:

"Your column is swell and I enjoy reading it very much, but who in h— has money enough these days to try one of your recipes? Your recipes are meant for the rich. Why not try to please most of your readers by splitting up your column, one expensive dish and one cheap dish, so we all may read and learn? Please think this over. Still saying your column is good, I am, Yours very truly, R. B. C."

Thanks to you, my good Long Island friend, for your constructive criticism. I'll go you one better and will devote the entire column today to the preparation of inexpensive foods. Please remember that I have often said that expensive cuts of meat do not necessarily make the best eating.

It is true that Rector's had a great many classic dishes on the menu to please its fastidious patrons, but you should have dropped into the kitchen when the chef and his cooks sat down to eat. There were no fillets of Mignon nor breasts of chicken a la Melba or a la something else but instead ragouts, savory stews, pot roast, and goulash were some of the favorite foods of these cooks. Each and every one of these dishes calls for inexpensive cuts of meat.

A few years ago I conducted a lengthy research into the preparation of inexpensive foods and it is with a great deal of pleasure that I now offer a few of them to you.

RAGOUT OF BEEF, BOURGEOISE.

Have the butcher cut two pounds of boneless chuck into uniform edible-sized pieces and ask for a piece of beef suet. Render suet in hot skillet. Meanwhile season meat with salt and pepper and dredge lightly with flour. Put meat in skillet and brown quickly on all sides. When meat is browned remove suet or surplus fat and add two cups of hot water, or beef tripe stock, stock if you have some on hand. Bring to boiling point; add one bay leaf, one bunch of carrots cut in dice, or if they are small carrots they may be left whole, 10 small white onions and potatoes cut in large dice or ball shape. Cover and simmer about two hours or until meat and vegetables are tender. Season with one-half teaspoon of salt, one teaspoon of Worcestershire sauce or any meat sauce you have on hand and thicken ragout with browned flour and water mixed to a smooth paste.

Browned flour is obtained by putting white flour in a heavy skillet which is then placed over moderate heat to brown, stirring until right color is obtained.

ROLLED ROAST, PROVENCAL.

Three to 4 pounds of rolled beef, 1 cup of chopped celery and leaves, 1 large onion (chopped fine), 1 clove of garlic (chopped fine), 2 tablespoons melted beef fat, 1 teaspoon of salt, ⅛ teaspoon of pepper, 1 cup of tomatoes, 1 head of cauliflower (separated), 1 tablespoon of flour.

Brown the celery and onion in melted fat, add the garlic and flour and stir until flour is thoroughly blended. Then add the tomatoes and the beef roll. Sear in a hot oven (450 degrees) for 10 minutes. Reduce heat to 350 degrees, season with salt and pepper. Cover roasting pan (self-basting) and cook one and one-half hours. Then add the par-boiled flowerettes and continue cooking until tender, or about one hour.

BEEF LIVER, CREOLE.

Cut one pound of beef liver into thin slices. Remove skin and veins and wipe with a damp cloth. Roll in flour and sauté in hot fat until browned. Then add one cup of sliced onions, one and one-half cups of canned tomatoes, two tablespoons of minced cooked ham, one green pepper sliced or cut into dice. Cover and cook slowly for 25 minutes, then add one-half teaspoon of salt and one-eighth teaspoon of cayenne pepper. Thicken with flour which has been mixed to a smooth paste with cold water. Bring to boiling point and let boil two minutes. Serve in a border of plain boiled rice.

HONEYCOMB TRIPE AND ONIONS.

Purchase two pounds of honeycomb tripe. Wash it well in cold water and cut into one-and-one-half-inch squares. Cover with boiling water, add one sprig of parsley, one sliced carrot, a tiny piece of bay leaf, a few celery leaves, six peppercorns, and one clove. Simmer very slowly until tender—about three hours. Meanwhile peel about 20 small white onions, cover with boiling salted water and cook until tender, or about 20 minutes. Also prepare three cups of cream sauce and flavor with one-third cup of tripe sauce. Put the tripe and onion in the cream sauce, bring to boiling point and serve.

ROAST FOREQUARTER OF LAMB, RECTOR.

Purchase a forequarter of lamb and have the butcher trim it and remove the bone for stuffing, the stuffing to be made as follows: Six cups of soft bread crumbs, 1 teaspoon of salt,

½ teaspoon of pepper, ½ teaspoon of sage, ½ teaspoon of thyme, 1 tablespoon of chopped onion, one tablespoon of chopped parsley, and ⅓ cup of melted butter. Mix thoroughly by tossing lightly. Stuff lamb, skewer the opening together or sew it together with thread. Place in a hot oven (450 degrees) for 20 minutes. Then reduce heat to moderate oven (325 to 350) and continue roasting, allowing 20 minutes to each pound. Baste occasionally and season with salt and pepper just before removing from the oven. Place lamb on a hot platter and pour off all but two tablespoons of the lamb drippings from the pan in which lamb was roasted. Mix two tablespoons of flour in the pan with the drippings and when thoroughly mixed, gradually add one cup of water and one-half cup of tomato juice. Stir over low heat until the boiling point is reached, scrapping and stirring all particles of meat essence well into the gravy. Remove from heat and season with salt and pepper, one tablespoon of lemon juice and a dash of Worcestershire sauce, and serve with the lamb.

January 27, 1939

In making my rounds of the markets, I came across two foods that particularly attracted my attention—domestic duck and lamb. Both are reasonably priced and of excellent quality, so I decided to avail myself of the opportunity and work out a new recipe for duck, and as for the leg of lamb—well, that would make its initial appearance roasted with fresh mint sauce. But the big idea back of the roast leg of lamb is lamb hash as it was prepared in the Cafe de Paris, Paris, France. This is a dish that both customers and cooks pronounce an epicurean delight.

I am often asked what one dish in particular do I like best? This, as you know, would be difficult for any one to answer, but I can truthfully say that lamb hash is one of my favorite dishes and I have taught thousands of people how to make it. I am going to give you the recipe today so the next time you have roast leg of lamb for dinner anticipate as I do the treat that will follow a day or two later. All I ask you to do is to follow the recipe closely.

It might be well to remember in French kitchens food choppers are rarely used, so you must use a sharp knife to cut the meat in very small cubes. It's going to take longer, to be sure, but the result will be different from meat that is emasculated.

LAMB HASH, CAFE DE PARIS.

Two cups cold leg of lamb, ¼-inch dice; ½ cup raw potatoes, ¼-inch dice; 1½ cup green pepper, ¼-inch dice; 3 tablespoons pimiento, ¼-inch dice; ⅓ cup finely minced onion, 1 cup lamb gravy, ½ cup tomato sauce or puree, ½ teaspoon salt, ⅛ teaspoon pepper, ¼ teaspoon paprika, 1 teaspoon Worcestershire, 1 teaspoon A1 Sauce, grated Parmesan cheese, butter, mashed potatoes.

Cut cold leg of lamb into very small dice, taking care to remove fat, gristle, and skin. Cover diced potatoes with boiling water (add a little salt) and cook for 10 minutes. Then add diced green pepper and onions and cook an additional 5 minutes. Combine meat, vegetables, gravy, tomato sauce and seasonings and heat thoroughly. Add a little of the water the vegetables were cooked in to bring sauce to proper consistency. Do not have sauce too thin, but just the proper thickness and quantity for a dish to be gratineed. Pour into shallow au gratin dish, sprinkle with grated Parmesan or Swiss cheese, dot top with small bits of butter and make a border of mashed potatoes around edge of dish.

Use a pastry bag to make potato border, but if you haven't one make a cornucopia of heavy brown paper, tear off half an inch at the point to make a large opening and squeeze mashed potatoes through the opening. Then with the prongs of a fork make a few swirls for decoration. In mashing potatoes for a border purpose add a raw egg yolk along with a little milk and seasoning to give color.

ROAST DUCK, ARMENONVILLE.

Have duck drawn. Remove all pin feathers, singe and wash thoroughly. Cook enough white potatoes to yield about one quart when mashed. Mash potatoes and season with salt, pepper, and one tablespoon of finely scraped onion and one tablespoon of fine chopped parsley. Whip all together, adding a tablespoon of butter and two egg yolks which have been beaten with three tablespoons of cream. Add a little more cream if necessary to obtain a light, fluffy mixture. Stuff duck with mashed potatoes, sew skin together, tie legs and wings close to body, dredge lightly with salt and flour and place in a hot oven (450 degrees) for 30 minutes. Then reduce heat to moderate and finish roasting, allow 20 minutes to the pound. Baste every 10 minutes during baking. Serve garnished with skewered fruit.

BAKED SKEWERED FRUIT.

Select prunes and apricots of the same size. Put to soak in cold water in separate pans about six hours in advance of the dinner, as this will soften them sufficiently for the oven cooking. Drain off water and dry thoroughly; remove pits from prunes. Fill skewers, alternating with prunes and apricots. Roll each skewer in melted butter and then in brown sugar. Place in a buttered baking pan and cook in moderate oven with the duck about 15 minutes, turning once in the cooking. Remove pan from the oven; sprinkle fruit with additional brown sugar, place under broiler flame until glazed and remove immediately.

If you are fond of duck and want something especially nice for your dinner try ducklings for a change.

BROILED DUCKLINGS.

The ducklings weigh about 2½ pounds. Have them cut in four pieces. Rub entire surface with softened butter, place on broiler rack, skin side up and cook under moderately slow heat until nicely browned. Baste occasionally and turn once in the cooking. Garnish with watercress and serve with a tart applesauce or current jelly.

RHUBARB MERINGUE PIE.

Filling. Three cups rhubarb, 3 egg yolks, 1 cup sugar, 2 tablespoons flour, ¼ teaspoon salt.

Meringue Top. Three egg whites, 6 tablespoons sugar.

Cut rhubarb in half-inch pieces. Put in colander and pour boiling hot water over and let drain. Beat egg yolks; add sugar, flour, and salt, which have been sifted together. Stir rhubarb into mixture and pour into well-lined pie plate and bake in moderate oven (350 degrees) until firm, or about 45 minutes. When cool cover with meringue, making sure that the meringue touches pastry rim. Meringue is made by beating egg whites until stiff, gradually adding the sugar and continue beating until fine grained and mixture will hold its shape. Brown quickly in hot oven, or under low broiler flame for one minute.

Under Pie Crust. Three-fourths cup flour, ½ teaspoon salt, ¼ cup shortening, cold water (about 2 tablespoons).

Sift flour and salt. Cut in shortening with knives (working in opposite direction) or finger tips. Add only enough cold water a few drops at a time to cut into a soft dough. Toss on slightly floured board, pat and roll out to circular form to fit pie plate.

February 3, 1939

Generally speaking there is very little new in the culinary art to write about. An interesting development, however, has occurred in the curing and smoking of hams which deserves mention.

I have become particularly interested in this new process which has brought about an outstanding achievement in flavor and tenderness of ham. You see, these new hams—and we will refer to them as new hams—are prepared and made tender and all ready for you to serve, with or without heating. No more old-fashioned scrubbing, soaking or boiling to get the ham ready for the table. Preparation requires minutes instead of hours to place this delicious meat on your table.

The time in baking a whole tender ham is amazingly short, as you will see when you read the recipe that follows. Ham is a most economical food, as every last scrap of it can be made into a tasty dish. Moreover, ham is good for breakfast, luncheon or dinner, and this fact alone should recommend the frequent purchase of a whole ham as an everyday household commodity. I hope you'll try one of these delicious, tender hams soon.

BAKED TENDER HAM.

Place whole ham on rack in baking pan, fat side up. Put in moderate oven (350 degrees), allowing seven minutes to the pound. Remove from oven, score fat, dot with cloves and pour over the top one cup of pineapple juice and one cup of corn syrup blended together. Return to oven and bake approximately 15 minutes longer, basting until ham is delicately browned. Serve with sauteed pineapple slices.

CREAMED HAM, RICE BORDER.

Wash ¾-cup of rice in cold water and drain. Cook in top part of double boiler with 2½ cups of milk until rice is cooked, or about 1¼ hours. Season with salt and pepper and stir in 1 tablespoon of butter. Pack rice into buttered ring mold, place mold in pan containing hot water and set it in moderate oven (350 degrees) 20 minutes.

In the meantime prepare the flour and gradually add 1½ cups of scalded milk, stirring constantly until sauce is smooth and reaches boiling point. Season with a few grains of nutmeg and add 1½ cups of diced cooked ham. Heat to boiling point, remove from fire, add 2 egg yolks slightly beaten and stir until thoroughly blended with the sauce. Season to taste with salt. Place a large platter on top of rice mold, invert and carefully unmold rice, pour creamed ham in center and decorate rice border with a sprinkling of finely chopped parsley.

HAM RISOTTO.

One cup diced cooked ham, 2 cups of boiled rice, 2 cups of canned tomatoes, 1 cup of broth (any kind), ½ cup of green pepper, minced, 1 teaspoon of onion, minced.

Cook the green pepper in the broth for five minutes. Add the tomatoes, onion and cooked rice. Bring to a boil and add the diced ham. Risotto is to be served moist but not watery, so if there is much liquid reduce it by evaporation with a few minutes of cooking. Season with a dash of Worcestershire, salt, pepper and paprika. Place a pat of butter on each serving. Very delicious and I am sure that you will agree with me.

HAM MOUSSE, EPICUREAN SAUCE.

Here is a recipe to use up the last morsels:

Two cups ham, finely chopped, 1 tablespoon of granulated gelatine, ½ cup of hot water, 1 teaspoon mixed mustard, ⅛ teaspoon paprika. few grains cayenne, 1 cup of heavy cream.

Put chopped ham in a bowl and pound with pestle until thoroughly mashed. Soften the gelatine in a very little cold water and dissolve in hot water and add to it to the prepared ham. Season with mustard, paprika, and cayenne. Add the cream which has been stiffly beaten, folding until mixed. Turn into a mold which has been dipped in cold water. Set in the refrigerator to chill. Unmold and garnish with parsley.

Epicurean Sauce.

One-half cup of heavy cream, 4 tablespoons of mayonnaise, 2 tablespoons of freshly grated horseradish. 1 teaspoon English mustard 1 tablespoon of tarragon vinegar, ¼ teaspoon of salt, few grains of cayenne.

Beat cream until stiff, stir in mayonnaise, grated horseradish and the balance of the ingredients which have been mixed together.

WELSH RABBIT.

One pound of American cheese, ⅓ cup of beer or ale, 1 teaspoon of salt, 1 teaspoon of mustard, 1 teaspoon of paprika, ¼ teaspoon of white pepper, 1 teaspoon of Worcestershire sauce, 2 eggs.

A well-aged and sharp American cheese should be used for rabbits. Shred the cheese and melt it with the beer over direct heat, stirring constantly until cheese is melted. Then add the seasonings and the eggs, which have been slightly beaten. Stir rapidly over direct heat for one minute. Serve on freshly made toast and have plates piping hot.

SALMAGUNDI SALAD (A COMPLETE MEAL).

To 2 cups of cold diced meat (lamb, veal, beef or pork) add ½ cup of cooked diced potatoes, ½ cup of cooked diced carrots and ½ cup fresh green peas or string beans. Put ingredients in a mixing bowl and let marinate with cup of French dressing, made with equal parts of vinegar and oil, seasoned with salt, pepper, paprika, a pinch of dry mustard and 1 medium sized onion chopped very fine. Marinate for 20 minutes. Then add ½ cup of chopped sweet pickle and 2 hard cooked eggs, chopped fine. Mix all together with 1 cup of mayonnaise, taking care not to mash the vegetables in the mixing. Arrange on crisp lettuce leaves and decorate the salad with cold sliced beets cut in diamond shape.

February 10, 1939

Some time ago I promised you a recipe for Napoleons, that delightful bit of French pastry that melts in the mouth. Many women shy away from making puff paste, but I want to take this opportunity now of telling you that it isn't at all difficult. Certain rules have to be followed and with a little practice one can acquire quite a professional technique.

When you master the making of a good puff paste you will be able to include in your recipes delicious tarts, turnovers, patty shells, rissoles, vol-au-vents and, of course, Napoleons.

PUFF PASTE.

Have ingredients cold, work rapidly, handle dough lightly and as little as possible. Butter must be washed for superior pastry and this is accomplished by placing butter in a mixing bowl, holding it under cold running water and squeezing with the hands until it is soft and waxy. Puff paste requires a hot oven and should be baked on a tin sheet covered with double thickness of unglazed browned paper.

One-half pound of butter, ½ pound of pastry flour, cold water (6 to 8 tablespoons).

Wash butter, squeeze and fold until all water is extracted. Cut 2 tablespoons of butter into the flour, add cold water and knead the dough five minutes. Roll to ¼-inch thickness, keeping paste rectangular and corners square. Place remaining butter in center of lower half of dough, cover with upper half and fold right side under and left side over. Roll to ¼-inch thickness. Repeat this process four times. Put paste in cold earthen bowl, cover over with a napkin wrung out of cold water and chill in the refrigerator for at least one hour. Cut into desired shapes, place on papered baking sheet and bake in a hot oven (450 degrees) for five minutes, reduce heat to moderate (375 degrees), and bake about 30 minutes.

NAPOLEONS.

Double recipe for puff paste. Divide in thirds and roll each third as thinly as possible and of approximate size. Prick each sheet with a fork before baking in hot oven (450 degrees). Bake until sheets are delicately browned. When cool put together as three layers, using a thick cream filling made as follows:

Cream Filling.

Seven-eighths cup of sugar, ⅓ cup of cake flour, ⅛ teaspoon of salt, 2 eggs or 4 yolks, 2 cups of scalded milk, 1 teaspoon of vanilla.

Mix dry ingredients, add eggs slightly beaten, add scalded milk. Cook 15 minutes in double boiler, stirring constantly until thickened, afterwards occasionally; cool and flavor.

Confectioner's Frosting.

One-quarter cup of boiling water, confectioner's sugar, ½ teaspoon of vanilla.

To the hot water add enough sifted confectioner's sugar to make of right consistency to spread; add flavoring.

Spread frosting over top layer of Napoleon, mark frosting to 4 ½ inches, and cut with a sharp knife.

Napoleons aren't always topped with frosting, but instead a heavy sprinkling of powdered sugar is used. Puff paste layers are sometimes put together with sweetened and flavored whipped cream. This, however, is a matter of taste. The important thing about Napoleon is the pastry. It must be light and tender.

RISSOLES.

Roll puff paste to eighth-inch thickness. Cut in rounds three inches in diameter. Place in refrigerator to chill.

Filling.

One cup of finely chopped cooked chicken, ½ cup of finely chopped cooked ham, 3 tablespoons of butter, 3 tablespoons of flour, 1 cup of scalded milk, salt and pepper.

Prepare chicken and ham. Make a thick white sauce by melting butter, blending flour and gradually adding hot milk. Bring to boiling point and let boil two minutes. Add finely chopped meat to sauce and season with salt and pepper. Place one tablespoon of the creamed mixture on a round of puff paste, moisten edge with cold water and lay another round of puff paste on top. Press edges together, place on a baking sheet which has been covered with two thicknesses of brown paper and bake in a hot oven. Serve with a well-seasoned tomato sauce. Smaller rissoles may be made by using one round of puff paste and folding like a turnover.

COMPOTE OF FRESH FRUITS.

Fresh stewed fruits make an impressive dessert, especially if one takes time to do them properly. When fruits are served as a compote they must be uniform in size, perfect in appearance and served whole. Peaches, pears, plums, cherries and blackberries make an ideal combination. Each fruit must be cooked separately (to retain its own flavor and individuality) in a medium sugar sirup which is equal parts sugar and equal parts water. The sugar and water are boiled together for five minutes before the fruit is dropped in. If a thick sirup is desired, then make it with two parts sugar and one part water.

The whole pears are carefully peeled, but a little of the stem is left on. They are then dropped into the prepared syrup and simmered until cooked or until easily pierced with a fork. Allow to cool in the sirup. The peaches are prepared likewise in separate syrup. Plums are not peeled, but are cooked with the skin left on the fruit. They do not require as long to cook as the larger fruit. Cherries are dropped into the prepared sirup and simmered for two minutes, saucepan is then covered and removed from heat. The retained heat of the sirup will finish cooking the cherries.

An assortment of the stewed fruits is served to each portion. A dish of sweetened whipped cream flavored with Kirschwasser is passed at the table. Make Kirschwasser cream as follows: Beat one-half pint of cream until stiff, gradually adding three tablespoons of powdered sugar and three tablespoons of Kirschwasser. Compote of fruit may be served with fruit sirup alone, but for a sophisticated dessert do it as we did in Rector's.

February 17, 1939

Do you experiment once in a while for new flavors in your salad dressing? Well, you should, because it's lots of fun to add a pinch or a dash of something to pep up the usual mayonnaise or French dressing. These two basic dressings should be made in quantity and kept in the refrigerator until needed.

There is no trick in making French dressing other than thorough mixing and accurate measurement, but with mayonnaise one has to take care. Mayonnaise dressing separates if the oil is added too quickly or if all the ingredients and mixing utensils are not cold. However, if the mayonnaise separates in the mixing it can be rectified very easily and be none the worse for perfect results. All you have to do is drop an egg yolk into a cold mixing bowl and gradually add the mayonnaise to it, beating the mixture until perfectly smooth. Select the salad oil you like. It may be French, Italian, or one of the fine American salad oils.

MAYONNAISE (QUANTITY RECIPE).

Four egg yolks, 1 quart oil, ¾ cup vinegar, 1 tablespoon lemon juice, 1 teaspoon salt, 1 teaspoon dry mustard, ½ teaspoon white pepper, ⅛ teaspoon cayenne.

Have the ingredients and mixing utensils very cold before work begins. Put egg yolks into large mixing bowl, add seasonings and mix thoroughly. Beat in the lemon juice and add the oil very slowly. When the mixture thickens add a few drops of vinegar and then more oil. Continue this way until all the oil and vinegar is used. Beat well after each addition of oil.

CURRY MAYONNAISE (FOR SHELLFISH SALADS).

Put one-half of curry powder into a small mixing bowl, gradually add one cup of mayonnaise, stirring until mixed. Also good when served with a chicken salad.

RUSSIAN DRESSING.

One cup of mayonnaise, ½ cup of chili sauce, 1 tablespoon of green pepper, finely minced, 4 pimiento stuffed olives, finely minced.

Stir chili sauce into mayonnaise. Add finely minced green pepper and olives.

THOUSAND ISLAND DRESSING.

Follow recipe for Russian dressing. Just before serving add one-half cup of whipped cream.

FRENCH DRESSING.
(Quantity Recipe)

Two teaspoons of salt, 1 teaspoon of white pepper, 1 teaspoon of dry mustard, 1 teaspoon of paprika, 1½ cups of oil, ½ cup of vinegar.

Put seasonings in a large bowl. Dissolve seasonings with a few tablespoons of oil, then gradually add a little of the vinegar. Continue adding alternately oil and vinegar until the quantity is used. Beat with egg beater until thoroughly blended. Pour into bottle, keep tightly corked in the refrigerator until needed. Shake well before using. I always crush a button of garlic and drop it in the bottle of French dressing. When used discreetly it becomes the hidden jewel of many an intriguing dish.

LORENZO DRESSING.

One-half cup of French dressing, 2 tablespoons of chili sauce, 2 tablespoons of chopped watercress leaves, 1 teaspoon of finely chopped pimiento, 1 teaspoon of finely chopped chives or onion.

Mix all ingredients together. Serve with mixed green salad.

VINAIGRETTE DRESSING.

One cup of French dressing, 2 tablespoons of vinegar pickle, finely chopped, 1 tablespoon of chives or onion, finely chopped, 1 teaspoon of parsley, finely chopped, 1 teaspoon of capers, finely chopped.

Stir finely chopped ingredients into French dressing. Delicious dressing for cold asparagus salad or cold artichokes.

ROQUEFORT CHEESE DRESSING.

This is a popular dressing among men when poured liberally over hearts of lettuce or romaine.

One cup of French dressing, ¼ pound of Roquefort cheese.

Cream the cheese by forcing it through a fine sieve, then gradually beat in the French dressing. This method of creaming the cheese will produce a thick emulsified dressing. However, if you like to see little pieces of Roquefort on top of the salad, don't use the sieve, but with the prongs of your trusty fork crumble the cheese until it is the size you would like to have it.

We mustn't forget our economical salad dressing that was developed in the Rector kitchen last spring.

SALAD DRESSING (MAYONNAISE TYPE).

Three-fourths cup of oil, 1 tablespoon of sugar, 1 teaspoon of dry mustard, 1 teaspoon of salt, ⅛ teaspoon of cayenne pepper, 2 egg yolks, ¼ cup of vinegar, 3 tablespoons of cornstarch.

Put oil in a mixing bowl. Mix and sift sugar, mustard, salt and cayenne pepper. This is important, as dry mustard is usually lumpy and this thorough sifting will prepare it for smooth amalgamation with balance of ingredients. Add sifted ingredients to oil, also add the egg yolks and vinegar, but do not stir. Add ½ cup of cold water to the cornstarch and stir until smooth; add another cup of cold water and cook over the low heat, stirring constantly until boiling point is reached and mixture becomes clear. Remove from heat and continue stirring for about three minutes. Pour hot cornstarch on top of ingredients in mixing bowl and beat briskly with rotary egg beater. Chill in refrigerator before serving.

February 24, 1939

The word "sandwich" got its name from the Earl of Sandwich. The story, as I am told, is that the Earl was so interested in gambling that he almost forgot to eat. The attendant, however, placed at his side a plate of sliced meat or cheese and slices of bread. He would quickly pick up a slab of meat, lay it on a slice of bread and start eating, all of which sounds reasonable and I guess true.

NEW SANDWICH BASED ON FRENCH TOAST. Speaking of sandwiches I thought you might like to know of a new one which has appeared in our midst. It is one that has evolved itself from the French toast idea—clever, n'est pas? I presume that you have all made French toast for breakfast and have found it a pleasant change when served with jelly, preserves or maple sirup. The French toast sandwich idea has many more possibilities, as any number of appetizing mixtures can be used from a simple savory butter to pate de foie gras. Suppose we familiarize ourselves with the making of French toast first and then we will go into the sandwiches.

FRENCH GRIDDLE TOAST. Three eggs, 1 cup of milk, 2 tablespoons of sugar, teaspoon of salt, 6 slices of bread (one day old).

Beat eggs slightly, add sugar and salt; strain through cheesecloth into a shallow dish. Cut bread in one half inch slices and remove all crusts. Dip each slice of bread in the egg and milk mixture, turning the slices until well absorbed. Brown both sides on a hot, well-greased griddle or frying pan. Remove to hot plate and sprinkle lightly with fine powdered sugar. Serve with jelly, preserves, honey or maple sirup.

FRENCH TOAST SAVORY SANDWICH (FOR TWO). Two eggs, 1 cup of milk, ⅛ teaspoon of salt, 4 slices of bread (one day old), 1 cup of grated American cheese. Currant jelly. Beat eggs and milk together; add salt and strain into a shallow dish. Cut bread in slices of ⅜-inch. Make sandwiches, using one-half cup of grated cheese for each one. Press sandwich gently together and trim off all crusts. Dip sandwich in egg and milk mixture in shallow dish, taking care to hold it together. Sauté in butter over low heat until nicely browned. Serve sandwich on hot plate and garnish center with a spoonful of currant jelly.

FRENCH TOAST SAVORY SANDWICH (FOR TWO). Two eggs, 1 cup of milk, ⅛ teaspoon of salt, 4 slices of bread (one day old), ¼ pound of liverwurst, 1 tablespoon of mayonnaise.

Beat eggs and milk together; add salt and strain into a shallow dish. Cut bread in slices of ⅜ inch and spread with liverwurst and mayonnaise which have been creamed together. Press sandwich gently together and trim off all crusts. Dip in egg and milk mixture, taking care to hold firmly together. Sauté in butter over low heat until nicely browned. Serve garnished with a sprig of parsley.

Now from this point on you can use your own ingenuity in making this type of sandwich. The only thing to remember is that the mixture must be chopped and held together with a little mayonnaise or softened with butter. Baked beans which have been forced through a sieve and the puree seasoned with salt and cayenne and moistened with mayonnaise make a delicious French toast sandwich. The garnish for this sandwich would be crisp broiled bacon or tiny pork sausages.

CREAM HERE EQUAL TO NORMANDY.

A few weeks ago I mentioned in this column Madam Poulard, who became world famous for her omelets. I have had quite a few letters since asking what was meant by Normandy cream which was specified in the recipe. Since Madam Poulard's unique inn was situated in the Normandy section of France, a dairy section which is noted for its excellent creamery products and eggs, she didn't overlook the bet of telling the whole world that the Normandy products were used exclusively in her kitchen. Don't let this disconcert you, as here in our own country we have just as good dairy products as Normandy, France. Our heavy cream is the equivalent of Normandy cream, which was specified in our text.

OMELET À LA POULARD.

Allow two eggs for each service or person. Break the eggs in a wooden bowl and allow one tablespoon of cream for each egg. Beat well with a wooden fork and season with a little salt. Heat the omelet pan and melt a piece of butter that will cover the entire bottom. Tilt the pan, as it is important to have sides buttered also. Pour in the beaten eggs and turn the pan over the flame so the omelet browns evenly.

There is a wrist motion in shaking the pan so the liquid part of the omelet will run over to the sides and under the bottom, thereby making a light omelet. If this motion hasn't been mastered or seems difficult, use a spatula and lift edge of omelet, letting the liquid part run under.

Cook only until omelet is set, then pour a little thick cream in the center and with the rounded part of a tablespoon smooth it out to the rim, taking care not to let the cream reach the edge of the pan. Take a spatula and with a quick turn fold the omelet and transfer to a hot platter.

The omelet may be served plain or garnished with jelly, thickened stewed tomatoes, sliced mushrooms cooked in butter and thickened, asparagus tips in cream sauce, chicken livers in a rich brown sauce, etc.

March 3, 1939

When I was a young chap my father took me to a restaurant in Washington, D. C. It was Harvey's restaurant on Pennsylvania Avenue. The proprietor, Mr. Harvey, was short, stout, and paunchy, but he knew food and enjoyed eating more than any person I ever met, hence he ran a mighty fine restaurant.

It was an oyster house and his kitchen was 100 per cent American. He employed Negro cooks and they were all trained by him. His oyster bar was famous throughout the land, and it was not at all unusual to see Senators, Congressmen, and members of the Cabinet sitting up on the stools at the oyster bar enjoying Harvey's steamed oysters.

The oysters certainly were a treat and never have I seen such liberal portions served—a peck of oysters was the portion. The delicious sauce which was prepared right before you helped more than anything in making this such a delectable dish. As a matter of fact the last half of the peck tasted just as good as the first half. My, oh my, what good eating that was!

HOW THE OYSTER MAN DID IT.

There was no secret about the sauce, but it was always uniform. In later years, I returned to Washington to take down notes on the making of the sauce, and here's the way the oyster man did it. The first thing he did was to set before me a small soup plate, sizzling hot. Into the plate he put two tablespoons of fresh butter, which of course, started to melt, and then came the seasonings—salt, pepper, paprika, and a tablespoon of Worcestershire sauce. Then three or four tablespoons of catsup and lastly a dash of tabasco sauce. All seasonings were stirred well with a fork—and then for the eating. Steamed oysters open easily and with a fork they are removed from the shell and dipped in the sauce. Before I knew it the whole peck of oysters was consumed with a final smack of real food enjoyment.

DEVILED STUFFED CRAB.

Melt two tablespoons of butter, add two tablespoons of flour and when blended together gradually add two cups of thin cream. Stir constantly until boiling point is reached and cook for five minutes. Then add two egg yolks which have been beaten together with one-half teaspoon of salt, a few grains of cayenne pepper, one teaspoon of dry mustard and one teaspoon of Worcestershire sauce. Remove from heat and add one pound of fresh or canned crabmeat. If canned crabmeat is used be sure to remove bits of bone and cut the claws in small pieces. Also add one-half cup of chopped cooked mushrooms. Mix all together and let cool. When cool enough to handle, stuff shells with the mixture, building it up rather high and rounded. Sprinkle with bread crumbs and dot with small bits of butter. Place in moderate oven to bake until crumbs are browned

ROASTED GUINEA HEN WITH WINE FLAVOR.

An enthusiastic reader of the column has asked me to give a recipe for roasted guinea hen wherein wine is used for flavor. I am very glad to give this recipe, as it was one of the outstanding specialties of Rector's Restaurant. When a guinea hen is roasted it is always cooked en casserole with the small casserole vegetables which distinguishes a dish of this kind. The bird was seldom stuffed, but was thoroughly picked and cleaned and trussed for roasting, after which it was rubbed with softened butter and a piece of fat pork was laid across the breast.

ROASTED GUINEA HEN EN CASSEROLE.

Select a young, medium-sized bird. Have it cleaned for roasting and go carefully to remove all feathers. Wipe with a damp cloth, truss as you would a roasting chicken and rub entire surface with softened butter. Put bird in casserole, cover breast with fat salt pork and start to cook in hot oven (500 degrees) for first 10 minutes, then reduce heat to moderate (350 degrees) and cook about 35 minutes longer, basting occasionally.

Small white onions and small potato balls (raw potato cut into small ball shape with a French vegetable cutter) are cooked in the casserole along with the guinea hen. If casserole is large enough add about one dozen medium-sized mushrooms at the same time, otherwise they can be sautéed in a separate pan and added to the dish later on. The idea, however, of a fowl and a vegetable casserole is to cook all vegetables and fowl together for a perfect blending of flavors. Fresh green peas are served, but they are always cooked separately in boiling water to cover (we put a teaspoon of sugar in the water), drained, and then seasoned with a little salt and pepper and moistened with fresh butter.

When guinea hen is roasted place it on a large hot platter surrounded with mushrooms, potato balls, and onions. Add one-half teaspoon of extract of beef to casserole and stir over heat until dissolved, then add four tablespoons of Madeira or Sherry wine, heat thoroughly and pour this small quantity over surface of bird. This is not a gravy, but a rich essence flavored with wine, therefore only a small quantity is needed.

BAKED ALASKA.

A solidly frozen brick of ice cream is needed for this recipe. Be sure that it contains no water ice. Cover a bread board or oven plank with a piece of white paper. Place a thin layer of sponge cake on the paper and then place the brick of ice cream on the sponge cake. The cake should extend about half an inch beyond the ice cream. Cover completely with a thick coating of meringue made by beating four egg whites until stiff with six tablespoons of confectioner's sugar. This is enough meringue for one quart of ice cream. Brown quickly in a hot oven. Slip from paper onto a fancy serving plate and serve immediately.

STRAWBERRY ICE BOX MOUSSE.

Two cups of strawberries, ¾ cup of sugar, ¼ cup of water, ½ teaspoon of cream of tartar, few grains of salt, 2 egg whites, stiffly beaten, ¼ pint of heavy cream, whipped.

Wash and hull berries. Mash and force through a coarse sieve. Put sugar, water, cream of tartar, and salt in a small saucepan and cook to thread stage (230 to 235 degrees). Pour hot sirup onto beaten egg whites, beating constantly mixture will hold a point, fold in strawberry pulp and whipped cream. Turn into refrigerator tray and freeze at least one hour before serving. Use raspberries or blackberries when in season in place of strawberries. Strain blackberry pulp through fine sieve to eliminate seeds.

March 10, 1939

Food properly seasoned is an art in itself. Salt and pepper are the basic seasonings and should be used during the cooking of the food, not after the food is cooked. A good cook in the home should study the tastes of the members of the family, so that no additional salt and pepper should be added when the food is placed on the table.

Many times I have watched a diner sprinkle salt and pepper on hie food before he even tasted it. Well, of course, that is purely a habit; and it reminds me of a small restaurant in Paris, Maison Montagne. The proprietor is Monsieur Prosper Montagne. He is also the chef. I am not sure whether he is among the living today, but a generation ago he was a great authority on culinary matters. He worked enthusiastically in his kitchen, which was separated from the dining room by a curtain.

When a party entered his restaurant and ordered one of his specialties, he would take his post behind the curtain as the waiter was serving the food. He would watch closely the mobile features of his guests, and if they registered approval, Monsieur Montagne would chuckle happily, but if the facial expressions indicated disappointment, Monsieur Montagne would leap through the curtains and remove the food.

He would then prepare another one of his specialties, and even another one, until his guests were perfectly satisfied. His great boast was that no patron ever left his restaurant disappointed or dissatisfied. He must have been the author of that well-known slogan, "The customer is always right."

SWEETBREADS NEWBURG.

Sweetbreads are purchased by the pair. Separate them and soak in cold water for one hour. Then cover them with boiling salted water to which has been added ¼ cup of vinegar; simmer for 20 minutes. Drain and plunge into cold water to harden. Remove any pieces of windpipe and membrane and cut into edible sized pieces. To 2 cups of sweetbreads prepare the following sauce: Melt 2 tablespoons of butter in saucepan, blend in 1 tablespoon of flour and gradually add ½ pint of cream, stirring constantly until smooth and boiling point is reached. Season to taste with salt and a few grains of cayenne, add sweetbreads and hold over low heat until thoroughly heated. Just before serving add 3 tablespoons of sherry wine. Serve in patty shells or on freshly made toast.

WIENER SCHNITZEI

One veal cutlet (cut thick), salt and pepper, 1 egg, 1 cup fine dry bread crumbs, hot fat or butter.

Cut veal into pieces for individual service; discard bone. Season meat with salt and pepper and roll each piece in fine bread crumbs, then in beaten egg and again in bread crumbs. Cook veal in hot skillet until nicely browned on both sides. Use only enough fat to keep meat from sticking to pan. Serve with a well-seasoned tomato sauce or a cream paprika sauce made as follows:

When veal is cooked and browned on both sides have ready to pour in the pan ½ pint of thick cream and one tablespoon of sweet paprika. Spoon the cream over the veal, heat thoroughly, and serve.

SOFT-SHELL CLAMS, MEXICANO.

Twelve soft-shell clams, 1 tablespoon butter, ¼ teaspoon salt, few grains cayenne; 2 shallots, finely chopped, or 1 teaspoon minced onion; ½ green pepper, finely chopped; 1 large, fresh tomato, peeled and chopped, and 1 teaspoon Worcestershire sauce.

Wash clams, open shells, remove clams and save liquor. Melt butter in saucepan, add clams and cook several minutes. Add seasonings, shallots or onions, green pepper, and tomato. Add reserved clam liquor and Worcestershire sauce and bring to boiling point. Serve with toast points.

BROILED SALMON STEAK, FINES HERBES.

Have the salmon steak cut ¾ inch thick. Sprinkle lightly with salt and pepper and dip in oil. Broil under moderate flame, allowing about twelve minutes for each side. Add a piece of butter to pan and baste during the broiling. When cooked place on hot platter and carefully remove the skin. Sprinkle each steak with ¼ teaspoon of finely chopped parsley and ¼ teaspoon of finely chopped chives. Add the juice of 1 lemon to the pan containing the melted butter and oil. Hold over heat for a minute or two until it is hot, then pour it over salmon steak. Allow about 2 tablespoons for each steak.

CHEESEWICH.

Cut one-day-old bread in fourth-inch slices. Thinly slice American cheese and make a sandwich. Season with salt and pepper and spread a light coating of mixed English mustard over cheese. Press sandwich gently together and trim off crusts. Sandwich may be left whole, cut in quarters or triangle shape. Melt some butter in a frying pan and over very low heat fry sandwich in butter until lightly browned, turning but once in the cooking. These fried sandwiches are delicious, but they must be cooked slowly and additional butter added to pan as it is quickly absorbed.

ORANGE CUSTARD.

One-half cup sugar, 3 tablespoons cornstarch, few grains salt, 1 pint milk, 2 egg yolks, ⅓ teaspoon almond extract, 3 oranges, ⅓ cup sugar, and 2 egg whites.

Mix together sugar, cornstarch and salt. Add milk and cook in top part of double boiler till thick, or about 20 minutes. Add beaten egg yolks and cook 1 minute longer. Remove from fire and add almond extract. Cut oranges in half and carefully remove sections with a small sharp knife. Place diced orange in bottom of shallow baking dish. Pour custard over fruit and cover with meringue made by beating egg whites with 1/3 cup sugar. Place in a moderate oven to brown. Serve cold.

March 17, 1939

French cooks have done more to develop sauces than all other cooks put together. I know that is a broad statement to make, but being around and among the best of them for only forty years has more than convinced me of this fact.

One of the fine French sauces most housewives are scared to death to attempt, but withal would love to master, is Hollandaise Sauce. Indeed, this is one of the most delicious sauces in the whole realm, and if the housewife can get the knack (it is really very simple) she will have something to brag about to her friends.

A real Hollandaise Sauce contains only the ingredients you will find in my recipe. I know that there are many recipes floating around under the name of "Hollandaise," but if you have eaten the real Hollandaise in a first class restaurant you would detect the difference.

TURN FOOD IN PAN WITHOUT USING FORK.
The word "sauté" which is used in French cookery is a French verb meaning "to jump." Now that is exactly what a French cook does to food when he fries it. With a certain motion of the wrist a French cook will take hold of the handle of the frying pan and jump the food in the pan to turn it without using a fork. This is easy, too, and with a little practice you can master it, if you want to.

The most important thing, however, about sautéing food is to retrieve the little essence left in the frying pan. This is accomplished by adding a piece of butter to the pan, after the food is removed to a hot plate, to loosen up those tiny particles that are the foundation of the sauce. Do not confuse the idea of this type of sauce which is served with a sautéed food as resembling gravy. Gravy is made by adding flour and water to the pan the meat was cooked in while sauce is made with meat essence and butter. Consequently it is much richer and only a spoonful is served with the dish.

Sometimes additional essence, which is known as glaze viande or meat extract is added to the pan when there is not sufficient to make a sauce. But then you know something about this, as I have frequently mentioned it in my recipes.

WOMEN REPORT SUCCESS WITH SAUCE.

About a year ago there appeared in this column my recipe for Hollandaise sauce. Since then I have received many, many letters from women telling me of their success in making the sauce. Well, that is exactly as it should be; and just one more word before we repeat the recipe, and that is to tell you that Hollandaise should be thick—that is, thick enough to hold its shape or about the consistency of mayonnaise. A delicious sauce to serve on hot asparagus, broccoli, cauliflower and fish.

HOLLANDAISE SAUCE.

Four egg yolks, ½ cup butter, 2 tablespoons strained lemon juice, ¼ teaspoon salt, few grains cayenne pepper.

Melt butter over boiling water in top part of double boiler. Meanwhile, beat egg yolks until thick and lemon-colored. Pour beaten yolks into melted butter and stir with a wooden spoon until mixture thickens. Add the lemon juice gradually, stirring constantly and watching until the sauce is of sufficient thickness. Remove from fire, add salt and cayenne pepper and serve immediately.

The secret of making Hollandaise sauce is the blending of the melted butter and egg yolks over low steam heat. Have only about one inch of water in lower part of double boiler and while stirring the mixture lift the top part of double boiler occasionally to allow some of the steam in lower part to escape.

It may never have occurred to you to do more than open a can of sardines when you fancied eating these small fish. Well, that's perfectly all right by me and what I have done myself on many an occasion, but here is a recipe I thought you might like knowing about.

GRILLED SARDINES À LA SEVILLE.

Select large sardines for this purpose. Drain off the oil and heat both sides of the sardines in a frying pan. Handle them carefully when turning them in the pan. Cut the bread the same size as the sardines and toast to a light brown; spread one side with anchovy paste (you can purchase this in small tubes) which has been mixed with a little finely minced parsley. Place a sardine on each piece of toast and return to the oven for one minute to heat. Serve with a drop or two of lemon juice squeezed over the top.

FRUIT ASSORTMENT IN UPSIDE DOWN CAKE.

Upside down cakes are popular family desserts and especially nice to behold if an assortment of fruit is used instead of just pineapple slices that we have had so much of.

Recently we made one of these cakes and the fruit we used consisted of two whole bananas (small ones), pineapple slices, peach halves, pear halves and cherries. When the cake was turned out of the large iron frying pan it was a picture, as the fruit and cake had taken on a glaze and this in itself is a mouthwatering sight. These cakes should be served slightly warm. Here is the recipe:

FRUIT UPSIDE DOWN CAKE.

Bake the cake in a large iron frying pan. Cut ½ cup butter into small pieces and put it in the bottom of a cold frying pan. Then sprinkle 1 cup of brown sugar over bottom of pan and arrange the assortment of canned fruit (drained of all juice) on top of the butter and sugar. Don't forget the bananas, as they give the cake a nice flavor. Cover fruit with sponge batter made as follows: Beat 3 eggs until light, add 1 cup of sugar and 3 tablespoons of hot water. Then add 1 cup of flour which has been sifted with 2 teaspoons of baking powder and ½ teaspoon of salt. Bake in moderate oven (350 degrees) 45 minutes. Remove cake while hot by inverting frying pan on cake plate.

MAPLE SUGAR TOAST.

Thinly slice one day old bread and remove crusts. Toast and spread lightly with softened butter and soft maple sugar. Return to the oven until the sugar melts. Serve each slice with a spoonful of whipped cream.

March 24, 1939

I suppose that if you want to be old-fashioned you will want to make your own soups, but with me it all depends. If I happen to have some good stock I certainly shall not pass up the opportunity to use it, which brings up the question, when is a soup a good soup? The answer is simple. It's the stock that gives body to a really good soup.

The same point applies to pies. It's the crust that makes a pie. The filling—well, that's easy. Of course, in Rector's, as in any other good-sized restaurant, there is usually an abundance of stock, both beef and chicken, but this is not so in the average home. It's up to the housewife now whether she wants to get soup stock the easy way or burden herself with plenty of work and expense.

This very situation came up in my home last night. I have a good recipe for making cabbage soup and had all the ingredients, except those to make the stock. So all I did was to open two cans of beef consommé which I diluted with an equal amount of water and then in a jiffy I had an excellent stock my cabbage soup.

Now supposing you have canned consommé in the house, but instead a jar of beef extract. All you have to do is to melt two tablespoons of the extract of beef in a little boiling water and then add and stir it into two quarts of boiling water.

The other day I received a letter from a lady living in Jal, N. M., who wrote me that she and her husband enjoy cooking and have used a great many of the Rector recipes to their complete satisfaction. Well, that is just fine and here is the recipe she requested for cabbage soup.

CABBAGE SOUP.

One and one-half pounds beef and bones, 2 quarts cold water, 1 teaspoon salt, 1 bunch soup vegetables, 1 bay leaf, ½-pound salt pork or ham bone, 1 small head cabbage, coarsely chopped, ½-teaspoon caraway seeds, salt and pepper to taste, thick sour cream.

Cover beef and bones with cold water, add salt and bring to boiling point. Boil briskly for five minutes, skimming the top of all froth. Add soup vegetables consisting of several stalks of celery and leaves, two carrots, one leek, one onion, several sprigs of parsley and bay leaf. Let simmer for three hours until a good soup stock is obtained. Strain stock into another sauce pan, discard vegetables and bones. To the strained stock add diced salt pork or ham bone, coarsely chopped cabbage and caraway seeds and simmer for one hour. Season to taste with salt and pepper and serve. Have a bowl of thick sour cream on the table and serve one or two tablespoons with each portion,

Salted codfish when combined with eggs makes a tasty breakfast dish. Try it for a change.

SCRAMBLED CODFISH.

Wash codfish in cold water and soak overnight. This will remove enough of the salt to make it edible. Never cut salted codfish with a knife but tear it or shred it with a fork. Beat four eggs and gradually add one cup of milk and one cup of shredded codfish. Turn into hot buttered frying pan and cook over moderate flame, stirring occasionally until eggs and codfish are set. Do not overcook, otherwise the eggs will be hard and dry. Garnish with parsley and triangles of fresh toast.

SWISS STEAK.

Have a thick slice cut from the top round at least two inches thick. Place it on a heavy board or table and with the rim of a thick saucer pound into it a goodly quantity of flour, or about one-half cup. While pounding turn the meat often, so that all the flour may become incorporated. Then season with salt and pepper and a liberal amount of paprika. Put one tablespoon of beef suet drippings in a hot skillet and brown one medium-sized sliced onion in it. Then add meat and brown on all sides, turning often. When browned pour in one cup of boiling water and one cup of to cover skillet and simmer until meat is tender or about one and one-half to two hours. Thicken liquid in pan with a little flour and pour gravy over steak.

BROILED LAMB CHOPS, CURRANT SAUCE.

Have chops cut at least one inch thick. Put chops on broiler rack and sear quickly in hot broiler oven. Reduce heat, or set rack three inches below, cook slowly 20 to 25 minutes, turning once or twice. Season with salt and pepper and as chops are placed on hot dish spread with softened butter.

Currant Mint Sauce.

One glass currant jelly (6 ounces), grated rind of half an orange, 1 tablespoon finely minced mint leaves.

Combine ingredients and with the prongs of a fork mix thoroughly. Let stand several hours before serving to impregnate jelly with flavor of mint and orange.

BAKED EGGS AU GRATIN.

Six eggs, ¼ teaspoon salt, ½ cup grated American cheese, 2 tablespoons butter, paprika.

Drop whole eggs into well-buttered baking dish, season with salt and dot with butter. Cover top with grated cheese and sprinkle with paprika. Place the baking dish in a pan of hot water and bake in moderate oven until eggs are set, then place dish under broiler flame for a minute or two until cheese browns.

ZABAIONE.

This is a delicious Italian dessert and is also a delightful bit of nourishment for convalescents. The real Italian recipe calls for yolks of eggs only, but there is a recipe wherein the egg whites can be used; this method is not the genuine Zabaione, but good nevertheless. The following quantity serves four:

Eight egg yolks, ½ cup powdered sugar, ½ cup sherry, marsala, or Madeira wine.

Beat egg yolks and sugar together until light and foamy. Turn mixture into top part of double boiler and cook over hot water, beating constantly and adding wine gradually. Do not have more than one inch of water in lower part of boiler, otherwise the yolks will cook instead of foaming. When mixture has doubled in bulk remove from heat and serve immediately in small-stemmed glasses.

March 31, 1939

The late Wilson Marshall was the owner of the famous three-masted schooner yacht, the *Atlantic,* that won the gold cup presented by the Kaiser for winning the race across the Atlantic Ocean. Before Commodore Marshall built his beautiful yacht, he also owned the two-masted schooner yacht, *the Atlantic.* This latter boat was purchased by my father and this good ship got its power exclusively from its sails. It had no engine. Among Commodore Marshall's shipmates was Augustus W. Mott. Mr. Mott was a bachelor, and a very rich bachelor at that, and died a bachelor. Now for the story.

The *Atlantic* had set its course from Block Island to Newport and immediately ran into an "Irish Hurricane," meaning, of course, not a bit of air was moving. The sails were flapping idly and the good ship was at a standstill. Mr. Mott had a swell idea.

He ordered the launch manned with the quartermaster and two sailors, to be steered over to a large number of lobster buoys. He told the quartermaster to stop alongside one of these and bring up the lobster pot. The quartermaster at first refused to do it, warning Mr. Mott that to disturb in any manner these lobster pots was a penitentiary offense. Mr. Mott assured him that he would take full responsibility.

In a few moments up came the lobster pot with three or four dozen shining, clawing, fresh live lobsters from the depths of the ocean. The quartermaster, at Mott's request, picked out six of these fine lobsters and deposited them in a box. At the same time Mr. Mott took from his pocket a bottle of fine old bourbon and around the neck of the bottle he attached his card securely with wire and dropped it in the lobster pot.

The lobsters were served for dinner that evening, and it is needless to say what a big hit they made along with the surprise of it all.

About two weeks later Mr. Mott arrived at his home in upper Fifth Avenue, and found a letter which read as follows:

"Dear Mr. Mott:
    "Thanks! Call again.
        "G. W. Perkins,
        "Owner of the Lobster Pots."

BROILED LOBSTER.

This is an ala Rector if there ever was one. We were the first to popularize these succulent beauties on Broadway.

Have lobster split and cleaned for broiling; also have large claws removed. Put lobster and claws on a double wire broiler, clamp handles together and broil under moderate flame having split part exposed to flame for 20 minutes. Remove to large platter; crack claws around heavy part of shell, season with salt and paprika and pour a little melted butter over all. Serve with additional melted butter and quartered lemon. Some like a little chili sauce and a few drops of Worcestershire stirred into the very hot melted butter which is good, but entirely a matter of taste.

LOBSTER THERMIDOR.

Here is another lobster recipe that we introduced to Broadway. It is just 37 years ago that I learned to make this dish in the kitchen of the famous cafe de Paris in France.

Split a cold boiled lobster lengthwise, remove meat and chop in very small pieces. Prepare a cream sauce as follows: Melt one tablespoon of butter, blend in one tablespoon of flour and gradually add three quarters cup of cream, stirring constantly until sauce reaches boiling point. Let boil two minutes. add one teaspoon of English mustard, one quarter teaspoon of salt and a few grains of cayenne, also add one quarter cup of finely chopped cooked mushrooms. Add chopped lobster meat to sauce, mix well. Fill empty lobster shells with mixture, building it up rather high, sprinkle over with grated Parmesan cheese and place under moderate broiler flame to brown.

CHICKEN CACCIOTORA.

One frying chicken, salt and pepper, flour, ¼ cup olive oil, 4 whole small onions, 1 green pepper, chopped fine, 1 pimiento, chopped fine, 1 clove garlic, minced, 1 cup canned tomatoes, 1 cup sliced mushrooms.

Cut chicken into pieces for serving. Season with salt and pepper and dredge lightly with flour. Heat olive oil in skillet, brown chicken thoroughly on all sides. Then add onions, green pepper, pimiento, garlic and canned tomatoes; season with salt and pepper, cover and simmer gently for one and one-half hours. Then add the sliced mushrooms and simmer for 30 minutes longer.

POTATOES AU GRATIN.

This recipe is to be made from hot boiled potatoes. This may sound odd, but try it. The result will be softer, fluffier potatoes than cold potatoes warmed in a hot sauce. For every two cups of hot chopped potatoes allow one and one-half cups of Veloute sauce made as follows: Melt two tablespoons of butter, blend in one and one-half tablespoons of flour and gradually add one and one-half cups of chicken broth (strained), stirring constantly until smooth and boiling point is reached. Add potatoes to sauce, season with salt and pepper and pour into a shallow with grated cheese and bake in a hot oven until browned.

GLAZED APPLES À LA RECTOR.

Six apples, 1½ cups sugar, 1½ cups water, 2 tablespoons seeded raisins, 2 tablespoons chopped walnuts, grated rind of 1 lemon. Mix together.

Add water to sugar; bring to boiling point and boil for five minutes. Then add apples, which have been peeled and cored. Cook until apples are soft, turning frequently. Care must be taken that apples hold shape. Remove apples to a baking dish; fill centers with raisins, walnuts, and rind. Sprinkle apples generously with sugar and bake in a moderate oven until well glazed. Meanwhile boil the sirup the apples were cooked in until reduced to one-half the quantity. Pour this sirup around the apples when they leave the oven. To be served hot or cold, with or without cream.

Also Available // CoachwhipBooks.com

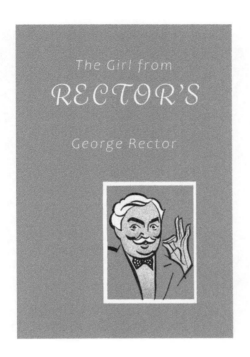

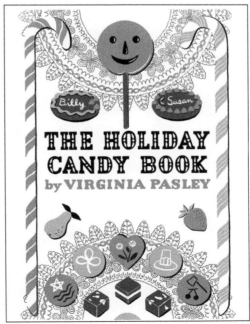

Also Available

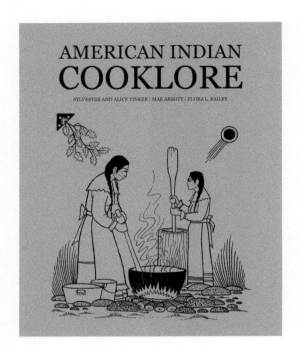

CoachwhipBooks.com

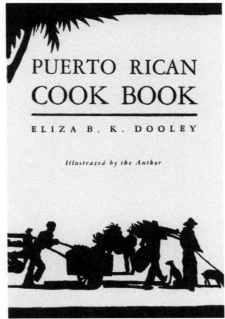

Also Available

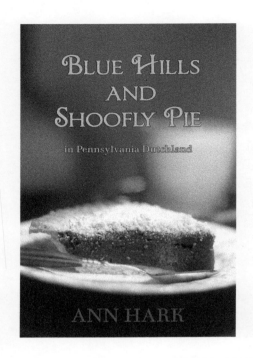

CoachwhipBooks.com

Milton Keynes UK
Ingram Content Group UK Ltd.
UKHW040259181024
449757UK00001B/142